TIMESAVER FOR EXAI

PHOTOCOPIABLE

IELTS Vocabulary
(5.5–7.5)

By Julie Moore

■SCHOLASTIC

IELTS VOCABULARY (5.5-7.5)

Contents

Title	Exam focus	Topic vocabulary	Lexical focus	Exam task	Page
All about image	Reading	Image and appearance	Synonyms	Multiple choice	6
Telling tales	Reading	Stories and narratives	Paraphrasing	Sentence completion	8
A matter of perspective	Reading	Art and form	Prefixes and suffixes	*True, false* or *not given*	10
In touch	Reading	Communication	Phrases and phrasal verbs	Matching features	12
Just a game	Reading	Sports	Idioms and metaphors	Matching information	14
New to science	Reading	Wildlife and nature	Noun phrases	Note completion	16
Caffeine kick	Reading	Health	Cause and effect	Matching sentence endings	18
Out of this world	Reading	Science	Fact and opinion	Identifying claims in a text: *yes, no, not given*	20
Crash test dummies	Reading	Engineering and technology	Multiple meanings	Diagram label completion	22
A way of life	Reading	Culture and tradition	Synonyms and antonyms	Short answer questions	24
Crime fighters	Reading	Crime and policing	Verb patterns	Summary completion	26
Making music, making money	Reading	Business and finance	Meaning and context	Multiple selection	28
Figure it out!	Writing Task 1	Describing graphs, charts and diagrams	Describing significant features	Describing a graph, chart or diagram	30
Pick a number	Writing Task 1	Expressing numbers and statistics	Compound adjectives with numbers	Describing data presented in texts	32
Trending	Writing Task 1	Describing trends	Word forms	Describing trends on a graph	34
The same but different	Writing Task 1	Making comparisons	Comparative adjectives	Comparing two sets of data in a graph	36
What comes next?	Writing Task 1	Describing a process	Sequencing	Describing a process from a diagram	38
In your own words	Writing Task 1	Expanding on and rewording labels	Collocations	Summarising a graph	40

Title	Exam focus	Topic vocabulary	Lexical focus	Exam task	Page
Who's who?	Writing Task 2	Describing people and groups	Synonyms	Essay	42
No magic bullet	Writing Task 2	Describing problems and solutions	Noun phrases, hedging language	Essay	44
A matter of opinion	Writing Task 2	Expressing opinions	Noun and adjective forms	Single paragraph of an essay	46
Who's to blame?	Writing Task 2	Talking about cause and effect	Active and passive verb forms	Essay	48
A case in point	Writing Task 2	Giving examples	Giving relevant supporting examples	Single paragraph of an essay	50
To sum up	Writing Task 2	Summarising and concluding	Avoiding overgeneralization	Concluding paragraph	52
All about me	Speaking	Talking about family, friends and home	Adjective + noun collocations	Part 1	54
What are you up to?	Speaking	Talking about work, studies and interests	Phrasal verbs	Part 1	56
Love it or hate it	Speaking	Talking about likes and dislikes	Positive and negative adjectives	Part 1	58
A funny thing happened …	Speaking	Describing anecdotes and past experiences	Colligation	Part 2	60
As a rule	Speaking	Talking about what's typical or general	Exceptions	Parts 2 & 3	62
And then my mind went blank!	Speaking	Talking about what you don't know	Adverbials	Parts 1, 2 & 3	64
The pros and cons	Speaking	Talking about advantages and disadvantages	Synonyms and paraphrasing	Part 3	66
This is what I think …	Speaking	Expressing opinions	Acknowledging other viewpoints	Part 3	68
The important thing is …	Speaking	Talking about what is important	Emphatic adverbs	Part 3	70
The odds are …	Speaking	Expressing uncertainty	Hedging language	Part 3	72

IELTS VOCABULARY (5.5-7.5)

Introduction

Who is this book for?

This book is for teachers of students preparing for the Academic modules of the IELTS test, and who are aiming for a score of 5.5–7.5. It is an ideal supplement to any IELTS preparation coursebook, especially for students who already have a good grounding in English. The topics and activities reflect those typical of the IELTS Academic test and are designed especially to appeal to young adults. This resource is also suitable for use with any upper-intermediate or advanced classes who wish to broaden their vocabulary, especially with a view to academic study.

The IELTS test – an overview

The International English Language Testing System (IELTS) is a test that measures the language proficiency of people who want to study or work in environments where English is used as a language of communication. An easy-to-use 9-band scale clearly identifies proficiency level, from non-user (band score 1) through to expert (band score 9).

IELTS is available in two test formats – Academic or General Training – and provides a valid and accurate assessment of the four language skills: listening, reading, writing and speaking. This Timesaver title focuses on the Academic modules of the test.

There are four components to the test.

Reading   60 minutes.
There are three texts with 40 questions in total.

Writing   60 minutes.
There are two writing tasks. Task 1 requires a minimum of 150 words. Task 2 requires a minimum of 250 words.

Listening   30 minutes (plus 10 minutes for transferring answers).
There are four sections with 40 questions in total.

Speaking   11-14 minutes.
There are three parts.

Each component of the test is given a band score. The average of the four scores produces the overall band score. You do not pass or fail IELTS; you simply receive a score.

BAND SCORE	SKILL LEVEL	DESCRIPTION
9	Expert user	The test taker has fully operational command of the language. Their use of English is appropriate, accurate and fluent, and shows complete understanding.
8	Very good user	The test taker has fully operational command of the language with only occasional unsystematic inaccuracies and inappropriate usage. They may misunderstand some things in unfamiliar situations. They handle complex and detailed argumentation well.
7	Good user	The test taker has operational command of the language, though with occasional inaccuracies, inappropriate usage and misunderstandings in some situations. They generally handle complex language well and understand detailed reasoning.
6	Competent user	The test taker has an effective command of the language despite some inaccuracies, inappropriate usage and misunderstandings. They can use and understand fairly complex language, particularly in familiar situations.
5	Modest user	The test taker has a partial command of the language and copes with overall meaning in most situations, although they are likely to make many mistakes. They should be able to handle basic communication in their own field.
4	Limited user	The test taker's basic competence is limited to familiar situations. They frequently show problems in understanding and expression. They are not able to use complex language.
3	Extremely limited user	The test taker conveys and understands only general meaning in very familiar situations. There are frequent breakdowns in communication.
2	Intermittent user	The test taker has great difficulty understanding spoken and written English.
1	Non-user	The test taker has no ability to use the language except a few isolated words.

For full details on the IELTS test, go to: **www.ielts.org**

How do I use this book?

The book is divided into three sections which reflect the three parts of the test for which vocabulary knowledge is particularly key: Reading, Writing and Speaking. However, the vocabulary may be useful across all areas of the test. Use the lessons to supplement your coursebook by providing extra practice of particular parts of the test or topic areas. The activities also provide thorough practice of exam skills.

- The activities are designed to be teacher-led but are used without separate Teacher's notes. Clear instructions are on the pages, which are all photocopiable.

- The test section, question type and lesson focus are clearly labelled in each lesson.

- The lessons have been designed to cover one hour of class time, depending on class size and language level.

- The comprehensive answer key at the back of the book provides explanations of the answers.

- Some activities ask students to work in pairs or groups to encourage them to engage with the language. These can be adapted depending on context and class size.

- The final activity in each lesson in the writing section is a writing task. Some of these require students to write a short answer of one or two paragraphs, others ask them to write a complete essay. These tasks are ideal to set as homework.

How important is vocabulary acquisition in exam success?

The IELTS test requires students to have a wide vocabulary including everyday, conversational language and the more formal language typical of academic reading and writing. In the Speaking and Writing tests, a proportion of the marks is awarded specifically for lexical resource. The activities in this book provide practice to help both broaden and deepen students' lexical knowledge across a range of skills and topics.

- For the Reading test, students read authentic texts which contain a wide range of vocabulary. In order to answer the test questions, students will often need to understand specific words and phrases used in the text as well as the overall message. The lessons in the Reading section focus on students' receptive knowledge of vocabulary, i.e. understanding vocabulary they encounter. The activities expose them to language typical of texts used in the Academic Reading test. Some of the vocabulary may be familiar but need consolidation and some of it may be new.

There are also tips and activities to help students practise working out the meaning of unfamiliar words in a text.

- In the Writing test, students are required to use a wide range of lexical resource. Students need to use vocabulary in the two writing tasks which is relevant to the topic and that is appropriate in style for a piece of academic writing. They need to use vocabulary in an accurate and natural way; choosing appropriate collocations, dependent prepositions, correct parts of speech, etc. Finally, they need to demonstrate a variety of expression that avoids repetition of the same words and phrases throughout a task, so a knowledge of synonyms and other forms of paraphrase is essential. The lessons in the Writing section provide practice of useful vocabulary around popular exam topics as well as specific functional themes, such as describing trends or expressing cause and effect relationships.

- In the Speaking test, students need the vocabulary at their fingertips to express ideas on a range of topics that might crop up. Again, marks in this part of the test are awarded for lexical resource, which includes range and appropriacy of vocabulary usage, as well as the ability to successfully get around any gaps in their vocabulary. The lessons in this section focus on a vernacular style of vocabulary to talk about the types of topics that typically arise. Each of the lessons is relevant to a particular section of the Speaking test and activities provide practice of a range of appropriate vocabulary and expressions, often through pairwork, which reflects the format of the test.

The Timesaver series

The Timesaver series provides hundreds of ready-made lessons for all language levels and age groups, covering skills work, language practice and cross-curricular and cross-cultural material. See the full range of print and digital resources at: **www.scholastic.co.uk/elt**

VOCABULARY FOR READING — Image and appearance — Synonyms

All about image

1 Work in groups. Discuss the questions.
- Do you take selfies?
- What's your favourite selfie technique? Do you use a selfie stick?
- Do you post selfies on social media?
- Do you think selfies are a relatively new phenomenon?

2 Read the text. Who are the two people in the pictures and when were they painted?

BEYOND THE SELFIE

Self-portrait at the Age of 63

Artists in every era show rich details about their lives and work through self-portraits

How do you select the selfies you put on Instagram? You might think about your facial expression, your hairstyle, and even what you're wearing. Each of these details says something about you to the people who look at your page. Knowing this, you probably make careful choices about the pictures you post.

Posting selfies is a recent phenomenon. But how people choose to represent themselves is not. Self-portraits, from all periods in history, are documents of the choices artists make about how to present themselves to others. From their clothing to the colour scheme and the composition, every detail in a self-portrait has meaning.

Dutch artist Rembrandt van Rijn painted nearly 100 self-portraits during his life. These works provide a visual record of Rembrandt's technical development and ageing face. The example above, painted in 1669, is one of Rembrandt's last. He uses a realistic style to capture every detail. Recognised for his innovative method of painting light, Rembrandt uses highlights and shadows to draw the viewer's eye to his face. This emphasis on the artist's expression fills the work with emotional depth.

French painter Elisabeth Vigée Le Brun created the self-portrait below more than a century later, in 1782. From the folds of her clothing to the delicate feather in her hat, Vigée Le Brun uses rich colours and varied textures. Her formal attire seems out of place for someone in the messy act of oil painting. Do you think she really painted while wearing such fancy garments? Or did she choose to represent herself fashionably to make a statement about her social status?

Self-portrait in a Straw Hat

3a Find words or phrases in the text which describe ...

a) face: ...., ...

b) clothes: *what you're wearing*, ..., ...,
..................., ...

c) colour: ...., ..., ...

3b Work in pairs. Discuss why Elisabeth Vigée Le Brun is shown in the clothes she is.

Vocabulary tip

Writers often use synonyms, words with a similar meaning, to avoid repeating the same word. This can help you work out the meaning of unknown words. For example, you may not know the words *attire* and *garment*, but you can guess their meaning because you know the writer is talking about *clothing*.

VOCABULARY FOR READING | Image and appearance | Synonyms

4 Underline two synonyms of the word in bold in each extract.

A The project aims to <u>document</u> the lives of ordinary people in the early 21st century. We are using film and audio to **record** everyday encounters in homes and workplaces, hoping to <u>capture</u> a wide range of lifestyles and experiences.

B Political cartoonists **represent** well-known figures in a way that draws out particular traits. They might depict a political leader as a donkey, for example, because they want to present them as being stubborn and unwilling to change their position.

C The prize is awarded for **innovative** new ideas in the field of engineering. This year's focus is on engineering projects in the developing world. The judges are looking for original designs, especially those which make ingenious use of limited resources.

D As a forensic scientist, it's my job to be concerned with the individual particulars of a case. We carefully examine all the evidence available, from the **details** of victims' phone records to the minutiae of their personal finances.

E Many of the documents stored in the archive are incredibly **delicate** and need to be handled with extreme care. Archivists wear cotton gloves to avoid damaging the fragile paper. Some of the earliest records are on parchment scrolls which are too flimsy to be moved and are now protected under glass.

5 Choose the best word to complete the sentences.

a) The design uses a very simple colour *scheme / style* of black, white and grey.

b) If you look closely, you can see the individual *facial / visual* expressions of each of the characters.

c) She uses a very *authentic / realistic* style to make the viewer feel as if they are actually walking through the city.

d) His photographs are designed to elicit a(n) *deep / emotional* response from the viewer.

e) Visitors to the museum are able to touch the fabrics, so they can feel the variety of *textures / highlights*.

f) When thinking about the *composition / scheme* of a photograph, try not to put the subject right in the centre.

✎ EXAM TASK: Reading (multiple choice)

6 Look back at the article opposite and answer the questions according to the text.

1 The writer compares selfies and self-portraits because:
  a they both tell us about how people choose to present themselves to others.
  b they were both a popular medium of expression during their time.
  c they show how fashions have changed over the centuries.

2 Rembrandt uses light and shade to:
  a make the picture more realistic.
  b focus attention on his face and facial expression.
  c create a feeling of sadness.

3 Elisabeth Vigée Le Brun chose to present herself wearing formal clothes because:
  a they were what she was wearing to paint the picture.
  b they were delicate and colourful.
  c they were fashionable and reflected her social status.

Exam tip

Make sure you can find the correct answer to a multiple choice question in the text. Don't choose an answer based on your own knowledge.

VOCABULARY FOR READING — Stories and narratives — Paraphrasing

Telling tales

1a Work in groups. Each picture in exercise 2a illustrates a story. For either picture A or B, discuss your answers to the questions.

- Where and when do you think the story is set?
- Who are the characters? How do you think they are feeling?
- What do you think is happening in this scene?
- What do you think will happen next? Would you like to know more about the story?

1b Describe your picture to the class.

2a Read the text which relates to your picture. What is the title of the picture? How much did you predict correctly about the story?

A Grant's story within a story

American painter Grant Wood presents not one narrative, but two, in his 1939 painting *Parson Weems' Fable*. Weems wrote the story of a young George Washington (America's first president) confessing to cutting down a cherry tree, stating, 'I cannot tell a lie.' In Wood's painting, Weems pulls back a curtain in the foreground. He points to an image of his fable in the background as if telling the story. Woods assumes that most people will be familiar with Weems' tall tale. He includes key objects, like the hatchet and cherry tree. He also paints simple forms, giving the work storybook quality.

Parson Weems' Fable, Grant Wood

B Rockwell's realism

American painter Norman Rockwell illustrated many iconic magazine covers. His images are famous for their realistic style and portrayal of life in small-town America. In his 1958 work *The Runaway*, the details work together to tell a story – from the title to the setting, props, and characters' clothing. The handkerchief-tied bundle on a stick is a clue revealing that the young boy has run away from home. The police officer and diner worker lean protectively over the boy to form a triangular composition. This arrangement draws the viewer's eye and implies a dialogue. The figures' facial expressions add an element of humour and nostalgia to the story.

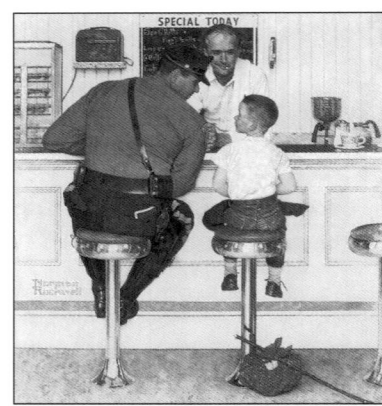

The Runaway, Norman Rockwell

2b Answer the questions about your text.

Text A

a) Who are the characters in the foreground and the background?

b) How does the artist include two narratives in the painting?

c) Is it a true story?

Text B

a) How do the props help to tell the story?

b) How does the artist show the relationship between the three characters?

c) In what way does the picture convey nostalgia?

VOCABULARY FOR READING   Stories and narratives   Paraphrasing

3 Match the sentence halves. Pay special attention to the meaning of the words in bold.

1 A **fable** is a simple story that …
2 It is a beautifully illustrated **storybook** …
3 Williams gives a convincing **portrayal** …
4 We're all familiar with that **iconic** …
5 The scene features a tense **dialogue** …
6 The old men sit over coffee telling …
7 The set design, the costumes and …
8 Her imagery evokes **nostalgia** …
9 The novel is a first-person **narrative** …

a) between mother and daughter.
b) **props** were all spectacular.
c) **tall tales** from their youth.
d) from the perspective of a child.
e) for times past.
f) aimed at 5-7 year-olds.
g) has a moral to teach.
h) of the 19th-century explorer.
i) image of Che Guevara.

4 Match the paraphrases to words in bold from exercise 3.

a) a moral story – *a fable*
b) telling of a story – ....
c) a conversation – ....
d) exaggerated or untrue anecdotes – ....
e) an illustrated children's book – ....
f) objects used to tell a story – ....
g) depiction of a character – ....
h) universally known – ....
i) fond memories – ....

Exam tip

Exam questions often test your understanding of paraphrasing and synonyms. Try to match the language in questions to sections of the text that have the same meaning.

Exam tip

Pay special attention to the instructions. If it says use 'no more than two words', you can write one word or two words. Use words from the text, and remember that the words you choose must fit grammatically into the sentence.

✏ EXAM TASK: Reading (sentence completion)

5 Read the text below. Complete each statement with words taken from the text. Use NO MORE THAN TWO WORDS for each answer.

Wyeth's Illustrations
American artist N.C. Wyeth painted nearly 4,000 illustrations for magazines and books during his life. Literary illustrations like Wyeth's bring words to life to help readers visualize the action taking place in the story. Even without reading the story, viewers can quickly understand the narrative in Wyeth's paintings, because they contain easily recognizable imagery. For example, in his 1926 painting *The Duel on the Beach*, the characters, setting and mood reveal the story behind the illustration. In this case, two pirates face off on the shore in a swashbuckling sword fight.

The Duel on the Beach, N.C. Wyeth

1 Pictures in books help readers to imagine how the events .... in the story might look.

2 It is often possible to follow a story just by looking at the illustrations because they contain .... that is immediately familiar.

3 In Wyeth's *The Duel on the Beach*, it is immediately clear that the main protagonists are pirates and that .... is by the coast.

VOCABULARY FOR READING — Art and form • Prefixes and suffixes

A matter of perspective

1 Work in groups. Discuss the questions.
- Do you prefer contemporary art or classical works of art?
- Do you have a favourite style of art? Do you prefer realistic or abstract pictures?
- Do you like the style of painting in the picture in the article below? Why / why not?

2a Which definitions of these two words do you think are most closely connected with visual art and painting?

perspective (noun)
1 [C] a particular way of thinking about a topic
2 [U] the way that far away objects seem to be smaller than things which are closer to the person looking at them
3 [C] the ability to understand the real importance of something compared to other things

dimension (noun)
1 [usually plural] the size of something expressed in terms of its height, width and depth
2 [C] a particular aspect of a topic
3 [C] the way that an object appears in space. If something is flat, like a square, we say it has two dimensions. If something also has depth, like a cube, we say it has three dimensions.

2b Match the example sentences to the relevant dictionary definitions in exercise 2a.

a) It's important to keep things in **perspective**. ....
b) We need to address this issue from a global **perspective**. ....
c) Social media has opened up a whole new **dimension** to advertising. ....
d) Shipping costs are related to the weight and **dimensions** of a package. ....

3 Read the article. How do photorealists use perspective to represent the world in three dimensions?

PLAYING WITH PERSPECTIVE

American contemporary painter Richard Estes shatters expectations about perspective

After the invention of photography in the 1800s, artists began to question their role in the world. After all, the camera efficiently translates the three-dimensional world into two dimensions. That was a job that previously only artists could do. In the 1960s, a group of artists known as the **photorealists** embraced the camera as an artistic tool. They began photographing their subjects, then creating extremely realistic drawings and paintings based on the photos.

American contemporary artist Richard Estes is one of the founders of photorealism. He is best known for his cityscape paintings of New York. To create a painting, Estes photographs a scene, then develops the composition based on the photos. Because the camera captures more detail than the human eye can perceive, the paintings are more vivid and the perspective more complex than could be achieved without using photos.

Cities are full of angles, lines, and geometry, which makes them the perfect subject for exploring perspective. In *Subway*, painted in 1960, Estes depicts the inside of a subway car using one-point perspective. The **symmetrical** composition is divided in half with the vertical pole in the centre. The left and right sides mirror each other, except for details like the advertisements along the ceiling and the newspaper on the bench. The lines created by the floor tiles, the benches, the windows, and the ceiling **converge** at the centre door behind the pole. This level of geometric specificity contributes to the hyperrealistic look of Estes's painting.

VOCABULARY FOR READING | Art and form | Prefixes and suffixes

4a Complete the table using words from the text. Check any words you're not sure about in a dictionary.

Noun	Verb	Adjective
a)	expect	
art / artist		b) ....
c)	compose	
perception	d)	perceptive
symmetry		e) ....
mirror	f)	
geometry		g) ....
h)	specify	specific

Vocabulary tip

Sometimes an unfamiliar word is a different form of a word you already know. You can often guess the meaning and part of speech based on the ending. Many prefixes and suffixes have a meaning. For example, *hyper-*: more than normal; *hyperrealistic, hyperactive, hypersensitive*.

4b Complete the sentences using the best form of the word in capitals.

a) People tend to _perceive_ images much faster than text. PERCEPTION

b) The placement of the black pieces exactly .... the white pieces on the other side. MIRROR

c) The traditional rugs use bold, ... designs. GEOMETRY

d) Flowers have a natural .... SYMMETRICAL

e) It is important to .... which colour you want on the order form. SPECIFIC

f) The exhibition far exceeded my ...., – it was just awesome! EXPECT

g) She hangs out with a fashionable crowd of ...., designers and musicians. ART

h) The images are .... of thousands of tiny coloured dots. COMPOSE

✎ EXAM TASK: Reading (*true, false* or *not given*)

5 Do the following statements agree with the information in the article opposite? For questions 1–5, write:

    TRUE   if the statement agrees with the information.

    FALSE   if the statement contradicts the information.

    NOT GIVEN if there is no information on this.

Exam tip

If you cannot find information in the text to say whether a statement is true or false, then answer 'not given'. Remember to base your answers on the text.

1 During the 19th century, photographers were first able to capture exact representations of the world on paper. ....

2 Artists didn't create paintings based on photographs until the 1960s. ....

3 Richard Estes is most famous for his photographs of New York City. ....

4 In Estes's painting, *Subway*, both sides of the picture are identical. ....

5 In the painting, the perspective lines meet at the centre of the door at the back of the carriage. ....

VOCABULARY FOR READING — Communication — Phrases and phrasal verbs

In touch

1 Work in groups. Discuss the questions.
- How do you keep in touch with friends and family – in person, by phone, by text message?
- Do you use social media? If so, which platforms do you use? What kind of things do you share?
- How has communication and friendship changed in the past 20 years?

2a Read the article. Which different means of communication are mentioned?

Is technology killing our friendships?

With social media, people can connect (a) .... each other more than ever. But some experts worry that we are actually more alone.

Kaylee, 13, has 532 friends—if you count her Instagram followers and Facebook friends. 'In one day, I can connect with 50 different people,' Kaylee says.
But some experts believe that for people like Kaylee, online friendships could actually result (b) .... loneliness. They worry that connecting online is not the same as seeing friends in person, and that kids like Kaylee are missing (c) .... on genuine friendships.

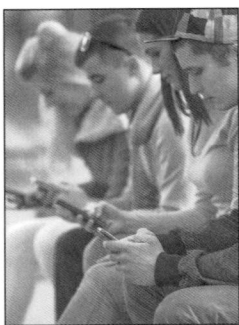

Alone together
When your parents were growing up, connecting with friends usually involved spending time together. When friends missed each other, they talked on the telephone. Nowadays, most communication happens online or through texting. Teens send an average of 2,000 texts every month and spend about 44 hours per week in front of a screen. Experts say that kids are spending too much time alone with their devices, and that this behaviour gets (d) .... the way of forming deep friendships. Larry Rosen, a professor of psychology, has stated that constantly checking online 'leaves little time for our real-world relationships'.
Rosen also worries that 'friends' on social media are not the same as true friends, because in tough times, you don't need someone to like your picture or share your tweet. You need someone who will keep your secrets and hold your hand.

Connecting with friends
Not everyone thinks that social media is harmful to friendships – after all, these platforms help people stay connected like never before. You can keep (e) .... with your friend who moved far away, watch your baby cousin grow up on Instagram, and stay up to date (f) .... hundreds of people. Online communication can make friendships stronger, asserts Katie Davis, co-author of *The App Generation*. Says Davis, 'Kids can stay (g) .... constant contact, which means they can share more of their feelings (h) .... each other.'

2b Work in groups. Find reasons in the article to support each side of this debate. Write them below.

YES Too much screen time is bad for friendships.
1 *People don't spend enough time together in person.*
2 ....
3 ....
4 ....

NO Technology isn't harmful to friendships.
1 ....
2 ....
3 ....
4 ....

2c Discuss which point of view you most agree with. Present your position to the class.

VOCABULARY FOR READING | Communication | Phrases and phrasal verbs

3a Complete the gaps in the article using prepositions from the box. Not all the prepositions are needed and some may be used more than once.

> at   in   on   out   to   up   with

Exam tip

Look out for phrases and phrasal verbs when you read. These may be paraphrased in exam questions using a single word synonym or another phrase with a similar meaning, e.g. *stay in contact - communicate*.

3b Match the question halves.

1 Is technology starting to get ...
2 Is it harmful for employees to stay ...
3 Are screen-obsessed children missing ...
4 Is it always desirable for us to stay ...
5 Could too much focus on technology result ...

a) in the way of face-to-face communication?
b) up to date with the news 24/7?
c) in relationship breakdowns?
d) out on other important childhood experiences?
e) in constant contact with their work email?

3c Work in groups. Discuss your answers to the questions in exercise 3b.

4 Complete the sentences using a single verb in each gap.

a) The survey investigated how much time teenagers .... online each day.
b) After everyone's checked their email and text messages and caught up on Facebook and Twitter, it doesn't .... much time for conversation.
c) You can always rely on a good friend to .... a secret.
d) The funeral was a difficult experience and it was good to have my partner there to .... my hand.
e) Some of the friendships we .... during adolescence can last throughout our lives.

5 Match the general words and phrases in the box to the sets of more specific items they describe.

> device   means of communication   relationship   social media platform

a) texting, telephone, in person ....
b) tablet, mobile, laptop ....
c) Instagram, Facebook, Twitter ....
d) friendship, marriage, network ....

✎ EXAM TASK: Reading (matching features)

6 Look at the statements of views expressed in the article opposite (1–5) and the list of people. Match each statement with the correct person A, B, C or D.

> **A** Experts   **B** Teenagers   **C** Larry Rosen   **D** Katie Davis

Exam tip

In matching questions, scan the text to find the key words from the options in the text. In this case, underline the names of the people, then identify what opinions they express. Remember that some options may not be needed and some may be used more than once.

1 Young people could feel lonely as a result of the focus on online relationships. ....
2 Too much time spent online is at the expense of time spent with friends. ....
3 Young people are at risk of not developing meaningful relationships. ....
4 Young people are now more able to share their feelings with others. ....
5 It is now easier for friends to communicate regularly. ....

VOCABULARY FOR READING | Sports Idioms and metaphors

Just a game

1a Do you take part in or enjoy watching any of the sports below?

> athletics   football   golf   gymnastics   karate   motor racing
> rugby   skateboarding   surfing   swimming   volleyball

1b How much do you know about these sports? Working in groups, discuss whether they are …

- individual or teams sport
- professional or amateur sports
- popular or niche sports
- spectator sports or mass participation sports
- Olympic sports.

> **Vocabulary tip**
>
> Sporting idioms and metaphors are common in English. 'Make the cut' is an expression used in golf. If a player finishes the first part of a competition in the top half of all the players, they 'make the cut' and can continue to the second part of the competition.

2a Read the article and choose the best subheading.

- Why golf should be an Olympic sport.
- How do new sports get added to the Olympic Games?
- Which sports will be added to the Olympic Games for 2020?

Making the cut

A Winning an Olympic medal is one of the highest honours in sports. In August, thousands of athletes were going for gold at the 2016 Olympic Games in Rio de Janeiro, Brazil. Along with competitors in classic summer sports like gymnastics and volleyball, you might have noticed the newcomers: golfers and rugby players!

B Both golf and rugby have previously appeared in the Olympics, but were removed in the early 1900s. A ruling by the International Olympic Committee (IOC) put these sports back on the roster for 2016 – bumping the total number of sports up to 28.

C Since the first modern Olympics in 1896, the IOC has made many changes to the games. Sports are often added or removed to keep the competition exciting. To be recognised by the IOC, a sport must have an international organisation that sets rules. But being recognised by the IOC isn't all it takes to join the Olympic lineup. To make this final leap, the sport must be very popular worldwide, and played by both men and women. Most importantly, the sport must reflect the Olympic values of friendship, respect, and excellence.

D However not all IOC-recognised sports have made it onto the Olympic roster yet. Skateboarding, surfing, karate are among those waiting for a chance to shine – and they may soon get it. This summer, the IOC will announce which (if any) of these sports will appear in the 2020 Olympics in Tokyo, Japan.

E Tom Scott, team captain for USA karate, thinks karate has a fighting chance. 'Karate is an exciting sport, and the discipline and courtesy required make it a great fit for Olympic competition,' says Scott. 'I think we've got a good shot.'

2b Work in groups. Which sport do you think should be included in future Olympic Games? Give your reasons.

VOCABULARY FOR READING — Sports | Idioms and metaphors

3a Choose the best word to complete the idioms in the sentences below. All the idioms appear in the article.

a) We want all children to **have a** *battling / fighting* **chance** of getting to university.

b) The site offers advice for employees who want to *do / make* **the leap** into entrepreneurship.

c) This event gives local talent **the chance to** *glow / shine*.

d) Lots of great ideas don't *make / take* **the cut** because the resources aren't available.

e) I think Anna *has / takes* **a good shot at** getting the job.

3b Work in pairs. Discuss the meaning of each idiom in exercise 3b.

4a Match the highlighted idioms in the sentences to their meanings.

1 The food was disappointing and the service was well **below par**; the staff were slow and unhelpful.

2 The banks keep **moving the goalposts** and making it ever more difficult for consumers to access free accounts.

3 The food retailer has finally **thrown in the towel** and announced the closure of all 500 of its loss-making stores.

4 We need to **keep our eye on the ball** and stay focussed on exactly what we're here to do.

5 The university needs to provide the resources and support to **create a level playing field** for students from different backgrounds.

6 The interview has been described by many as **an own goal** for the politician who far from winning support, has simply exposed his ignorance.

7 Solar power and biofuels were **neck and neck** in terms of investment last year, with roughly $170 million invested in each area.

8 It soon became clear that Tokyo was the clear **frontrunner** in the bid for the 2020 summer Olympics.

a) your own error that makes you suffer

b) equally successful or popular

c) not as good as expected

d) the most likely winner of a contest

e) to keep your attention on something important you're doing

f) to change the rules or aims of something in an unfair way

g) to give up

h) a fair situation for everyone

4b Work in pairs. Which sports do you think the idioms come from?

✏ EXAM TASK: Reading (matching information)

5 Re-read the article. Which paragraph contains the following information? Write the correct letter A–E.

1 The criteria for a sport to be included in the Olympic Games. ....

2 The perspective of someone from a particular sport. ....

3 Plans for inclusion at the 2020 Olympic Games. ....

4 The history of golf and rugby at the Olympic Games. ....

5 The total number of sports featuring in the 2016 games. ....

Exam tip

In this type of task, you are looking for specific information, not just the main idea of each paragraph. There may be more than one piece of information in the same paragraph, so you may need to use the same letter more than once.

VOCABULARY FOR READING | Wildlife and nature | Noun phrases

New to science

1 Work in groups. Brainstorm names of animals from your own country in each category.
- mammals
- birds
- insects
- reptiles & amphibians
- fish & marine life

2a You are going to read an article about new species of plants and animals. Before you read, guess how many different species there are on Earth. Write down your estimate.

2b Read the article to check. When you find the answer, stop reading and put your hand up.

STUNNING SPECIES
Scientists discover new creatures in surprising places

What do a striped frog, a rat-eating plant, and a poisonous, hot pink millipede have in common? They're all strange, recently discovered species.

Even after centuries of exploration, scientists are naming new species at a rate of 15,000 to 20,000 each year – with no sign of slowing down. 'We live on an amazingly biologically diverse planet,' says Quinton Wheeler, a taxonomist who classifies species at Arizona State University. 'So almost everywhere you look, species have found a way of carving out a living.'

Taxonomists have identified about 2 million plant and animal species. They estimate that another 10 million to 100 million remain undiscovered – and they warn that we need to find them fast. Habitat loss, climate change, and other issues threaten biodiversity – the variety of different species. 'We fear that we are losing species faster than were actually discovering and describing them,' says Wheeler. So the race is on to find new species and explorers are getting help from modern technology.

Little explored biodiversity hotspots are obvious places to search, but the challenge is reaching them. 'It's not too difficult to run across new species, if you're looking in places that haven't been very well studied,' says Laurence Madin, a marine biologist. High-tech tools helped Madin's team on a 2007 expedition to the Celebes Sea near the Philippines. He says, 'We used deep sea exploration robots – remotely operated vehicles that would enable us to go down to a depth of 3000 metres and look around and collect things without having to send a person down there.'

The remotely operated submarine relayed video to the scientists on the ship above. That's how they spotted the previously unknown squid worm – a bizarre-looking marine worm with what look like tentacles growing from its head.

Oceans aren't the only hard-to-reach environments that can be accessed with modern tools. Helicopters drop scientists into remote areas such as the mountaintop forest in Papua New Guinea where researchers found a lime-green jumping spider in 2008. And satellite imagery helps researchers plan their trips. Ironically, deforestation, or clearing away trees, sometimes leads to discovery, since logging roads open the way into previously undisturbed forests.

New species aren't only found in exotic places. 'People sometimes find them in places where they've gone all their lives,' says Madin. 'They just happen to look under the right leaf, or they happen to have the right type of instrument or microscope.' That's what happened in the US state of Georgia in 2007, when a researcher discovered the tiny patch-nosed salamander under a pile of leaves.

Squid worm

Vocabulary tip

Sometimes when you come across an unknown word in a text, the writer has actually explained its meaning within the text. For example, in this text, a *taxonomist* is someone 'who classifies species'. Writers also use noun phrases to get across a lot of detail. For example, *strange, recently discovered species* is more concise than *species which are strange and which were discovered recently*.

VOCABULARY FOR READING — Wildlife and nature — Noun phrases

3a Read the full article and underline explanations of these terms.

a) biodiversity   b) deep sea exploration robots   c) deforestation

3b 'Unpack' the meanings of the noun phrases from the article.

a) a rat-eating plant: a plant which ....

b) an amazingly biologically diverse planet: a planet which ....

c) little explored biodiversity hotspots: hotspots of ....

d) the remotely operated submarine: the submarine which ....

e) the previously unknown squid worm: the squid worm which ....

f) previously undisturbed forests: forests which ....

3c Underline examples of plants and animals mentioned in the article. In pairs, discuss what they might be like.

4 Match the highlighted expressions in sentences 1–6 to the paraphrases a–i. Not all the paraphrases are needed.

1 Some of the features that insects **have in common** are a body divided into three parts, three pairs of legs and large compound eyes.

2 A young blue whale gains weight during its first 6 to 12 months of life **at a rate of** 90 to 115 kilograms per day.

3 This upward trend has continued for 10 years now and shows **no sign of** stopping.

4 It's amazing how animals **find a way of** overcoming the most extreme obstacles to thrive.

5 As winter approaches, **the race is on** for many animals to build up reserves before the freezing weather sets in.

6 We were very lucky that we **just happened to** be visiting during the annual butterfly migration.

a) there isn't much time to do something
b) manage to do something difficult
c) to occur or exist
d) to be usual or frequent
e) to do something that was not planned
f) seem unlikely to
g) to be the same or similar
h) to be in competition with someone
i) at a particular speed

✎ EXAM TASK: Reading (note completion)

5 Re-read the article and complete the notes. Choose NO MORE THAN THREE WORDS from the passage for each answer.

1 New species identified annually: ....

2 Known species to date: ....

3 Estimated further possible species: ....

4 Maximum depth of deep-sea exploration vehicles: ....

Animal	Features	Location	Date discovered
millipede	pink, (5)		
squid worm	tentacles	the Celebes Sea, (6)	2007
7)	lime-green, jumps	Papua New Guinea	8) ....
salamander	tiny, patch-nosed	(9) ...., USA	10) ....

> **Exam tip**
>
> For any question that specifies the number of words you can use, numbers count as one word. 15,000 = one word

VOCABULARY FOR READING — Health — Cause and effect

Caffeine kick

1a Work in groups. Discuss the differences between the words in the box. Use a dictionary if necessary.

> beverage   caffeinated drink   energy drink
> fizzy drink   soda   soft drink   sports drink

Vocabulary tip

Some words are used differently in British and American English. In British English, *soda* or *soda water* is sparkling water. In American English, *soda is* any kind of sweet, fizzy drink, such as cola.

1b Write examples of drinks for the words in the box. They could be general types of drinks (e.g. *coffee*) or brand names. Some will fit into more than one group.

1c Conduct a short survey to find out what type of drinks members of your group drink most regularly.

2a Read the first paragraph of an article about caffeinated drinks. Why might some adverts be misleading?

Jittery drinks
Caffeinated soda and energy drinks might give you a boost, but they could also cause your grades to plunge

Commercials on TV make soda and energy drinks look appealing. They show people guzzling the beverages while playing extreme sports and hanging out with friends. But what these ads don't tell you is that too much caffeine, the chemical stimulant drug added to these beverages to give you that lift, could be harmful to your health – and your grades.

2b Find words in the paragraph that mean …

a) advertisements *commercials*, ...

b) a short-term increase in energy ...., ...

c) to fall suddenly ....

d) to drink something quickly ....

3a Read the next paragraph. What is the link between caffeinated drinks and poor performance at school?

Researchers recently found that middle school students who consumed even one energy drink per day was 66 percent more likely to show signs of hyperactivity. Symptoms of hyperactivity include a lack of focus, increased anxiety and heart rate, and disrupted sleep. This could be a big problem, because a 2014 study found that 73 percent of American kids consume caffeine daily.

3b Find synonyms in the paragraph for these words and phrases.

a) eat or drink ....

b) worry ....

c) insomnia ....

d) children ....

3c Which synonym in each pair is more formal?

VOCABULARY FOR READING | Health | Cause and effect

4 Work in pairs. Read the rest of the article. How do you think this issue could be addressed?

Caffeine complications

Jeanette Ickovics is a professor of public health at Yale University. She led the study examining the relationship between caffeine and hyperactivity in middle school students. She says her findings provide strong evidence that caffeine's side effects can cause symptoms that make it difficult for students to pay attention and do well in school.

To find out if there is a connection between hyperactivity and caffeine consumption, Ickovics interviewed more than 1,600 middle school students. She asked how many and which types of caffeinated drinks each student had drunk within the past 24 hours.

Then Ickovics asked each student a list of questions that could help diagnose hyperactivity. 'As the number of drinks went up, so did the number and severity of symptoms,' says Ickovics. She found that even one additional drink per day could heighten the level of hyperactivity in the students by an average of 14 percent.

Other findings from the study showed that boys are more likely to drink caffeinated drinks. Ickovics suspects that this is because companies market drinks with ads that are targeted at boys.

Sweet symptoms

The dangers of caffeine rich beverages go beyond hyperactivity. Each drink can also contain up to 40 grams of sugar. That's the equivalent of 10 teaspoons. The American Heart Association recommends that children limit themselves to 21 to 33 grams of sugar each day. Eating too much sugar could lead to an increased risk of obesity, heart disease, diabetes and digestive illnesses. 'So if you have one soda, you're already exceeding that daily recommendation,' says Ickovics.

5 Match the words in the box to the examples.

diagnosis   recommendation   side effect   symptoms

a) During pregnancy, women should avoid raw or undercooked meats. ....

b) These painkillers may cause tiredness. ....

c) The doctor said that I've got a chest infection. ....

d) She was suffering from severe headaches and dizziness. ....

✎ EXAM TASK: Reading (matching sentence endings)

6 Complete each sentence with the correct ending A–H.

1 The study set out to explore the relationship ....

2 The findings of the research provided strong ....

3 Ickovics found that consuming these drinks may lead to ....

4 The research also found that boys are more likely ....

5 Ickovics also suggests that these drinks could be damaging because ....

A symptoms such as anxiety, insomnia and lack of concentration.

B to consume drinks that contain caffeine.

C between hyperactivity and caffeine consumption.

D connection between caffeine intake and poor grades.

E of high sugar content.

F evidence of a link between caffeine consumption and hyperactivity.

G to experience severe side effects from caffeinated drinks.

H they contain high levels of sugar.

Exam tip

Check that each statement matches an idea expressed in the text. There may be more endings than you need.

VOCABULARY FOR READING | Science | Fact and opinion

Out of this world

1a Work in groups. Match the scientists to the new things they might find.

> astronomer   biologist   chemist   engineer   geneticist   geologist   pharmacologist   physicist

a) new species of plants and animals ....
b) new applications of technology ....
c) new materials and chemical elements ....
d) new types of tiny atomic particles ....
e) new drugs to treat diseases ....
f) new planets, suns and solar systems ....
g) breakthroughs in the understanding of DNA ....
h) new evidence of how the Earth was formed ....

1b Discuss which areas of science you think are most important or most useful. Explain your reasons.

2a Read the short extracts from four science articles below and match the headings to the articles. Which areas of science do they describe?

1 How to make an element ....
2 Man's best friend ....
3 Shark trackers ....
4 Superstorm ....

> **A** Each device has two special microphones that listen for sound waves underwater. The ping from the shark's tag as it passes by reaches each microphone at a slightly different time. An onboard computer uses the time difference to **calculate** where the shark is and which direction it's heading.

> **B** Italian astronomer Giovanni Cassini was the first to observe and write about Jupiter's Giant Red Spot in 1665. Since then, astronomers have determined that this giant spot is actually a storm in the planet's upper atmosphere.

> **C** Dogs and humans have a long history together. Scientists hypothesise that the first people arrived in North America about 15,000 years ago when they travelled across a land bridge that connected Siberia with Alaska. Dogs either came over with them or arrived shortly thereafter.

> **D** Scientists in Germany have made a smashing discovery. They recently confirmed the existence of a new element. The scientists created the element by using a machine that slams two atoms into each other at high speeds. The atoms combined, creating element 117.

2b Complete these sentences from the next part of each extract. Use a different form of one of the words from the text.

a) These _calculations_ help scientists to track the shark's movements.
b) Such .... by early scientists have been further refined using modern technology.
c) Scientists used DNA to study the ancestry of America's dogs in order to test this ....
d) The new element doesn't occur in nature, it only .... in the laboratory.

3 Read the article opposite about the search for a ninth planet in the solar system. Underline answers to the questions.

a) What hypotheses have been put forward about Planet Nine?
b) What evidence has already been found for the existence of Planet Nine?

> **Vocabulary tip**
>
> *Hypothesis* and *theory* have very similar meanings in everyday usage. In academic research, a hypothesis is an idea based on evidence - it suggests that something may be true. A theory is a more developed set of ideas that attempts to explain why. The plural of *hypothesis* is *hypotheses*

VOCABULARY FOR READING — Science — Fact and opinion

THE HUNT FOR PLANET NINE

Astronomers believe they've found evidence for a massive ninth planet in our solar system

Since the demotion of Pluto from full-fledged planet to dwarf planet 10 years ago, our solar system has consisted of just eight planets. But the story may not end there. In January, a pair of astronomers at the California Institute of Technology reported that our solar system may have a population of nine after all – and Planet Nine, if it exists, could be a big one.

Astronomers Konstatin Batygin and Mike Brown have been trying to solve a puzzle about objects in the Kuiper belt. This vast region of icy asteroids where Pluto resides contains some objects with strangely tilted orbits. Batygin and Brown recently realised that the likeliest explanation is that the gravity from a big planet has pulled them into their odd orbits. According to their calculations, the hypothetical Planet Nine should be around 10 times the mass of Earth and orbit the sun at an average distance of around 25 times as far as Neptune. If Batygin and Brown are correct, a single year on Planet Nine lasts 20,000 Earth-years! Brown, Batygin and others theorise that the planet may be an ice giant, like Uranus and Neptune. They also suspect that its orbit is very elliptical, or flattened into an oval shape, compared with the other members of the solar system.

Batygin and Brown hypothesise that Planet Nine hasn't always been exiled to the outer reaches of the solar system. They think it formed near Jupiter and Saturn at the same time as the rest of the planets, around 4.5 billion years ago. In the gravitational tug-of-war that took place as the young planets formed, Planet Nine probably got flung out to the solar system's hinterlands.

So far, observations of the objects with the weird orbits in the Kuiper belt are the only evidence for Planet Nine's existence. Some scientists are sceptical that it's real. But that could soon change: astronomers are racing to make a direct observation of Planet Nine through a telescope – now that they know where to look.

✎ EXAM TASK: Reading (identifying claims in a text; *yes, no, not given*)

Exam tip

In this task, you are looking at the writer's claims not at factual information. Match the statements to ideas in the reading passage. They will be paraphrases, so you will need to look for synonyms.

4 Do the following statements agree with the claims of the writer in the article above? Write:

    YES   if the statement agrees with the information
    NO   if the statement contradicts the information
    NOT GIVEN if there is no information about this in the passage

1 Astronomers Batygin and Brown believe there is a ninth large planet in the solar system. ....

2 Astronomers believe there may be other undiscovered planets in the Kuiper belt. ....

3 Batygin and Brown have calculated that the new planet could be much larger than Earth. ....

4 Batygin and Brown believe that Planet Nine formed in the outer part of the solar system. ....

5 Astronomers have observed the new planet using telescopes. ....

6 Other scientists have put forward alternative theories about the ninth planet. ....

VOCABULARY FOR READING — Engineering and technology — Multiple meanings

Crash test dummies

1a Work in pairs. Check that you can identify these parts of the body.

> ankle   chest   elbow   hips   neck   ribs
> shoulder   skull   pine   toes   torso   wrist

1b How do the safety features of modern cars help to protect drivers and passengers? Use some of the ideas below. Use a dictionary to help if necessary.

> airbags   anti-lock braking systems (ABS)   crumple zones   head restraints   seat belts

Example: Anti-lock brakes stop the vehicle's wheels locking if you brake suddenly. That means that the driver can keep better control of the car in an emergency situation.

2a Read the article about vehicle safety tests. Which …

a) parts of the body does it mention?

b) vehicle safety features does it mention?

One smart dummy

General Motors tests the safety of each and every vehicle design by using crash-test dummies. But the 200 dummies at GM's lab get battered and twisted even before getting in the car! Machines pummel the dummies to make sure their 75 sensors are working properly. These sensors record impacts that could occur to a person's body during a car crash.

A crash can be over in 150 milliseconds – less than the blink of an eye. The dummy's sensors collect data 10,000 times every second. This information is stored in devices embedded in the torso or legs. To predict the severity of head injuries, three tiny accelerometers monitor the speed and direction of the head as it slows after impact. Load sensors record how much vertical force and torque, or twisting force, the dummy's neck experiences. Each dummy has metal ribs with special sensors that measure compression of the chest during an accident. These measurements predict the risk of broken ribs and help fine-tune seat belt performance.

The newly upgraded Hybrid III crash dummy is used by car manufacturers worldwide for frontal crash tests on vehicles. The data collected from Hybrid III dummies over the years have helped improve airbags, seat belts and other vehicle-safety features.

'Cars are much safer than they have ever been,' says Jack Jensen, a GM safety engineer. However, he adds, even with technological improvements, the most important safety feature of a car is an undistracted driver.

2b What does Jack Jensen say is more important than the safety features that are part of a car's design? Explain why.

2c Underline phrases in the article which could help you work out what the words mean.

a) accelerometer

b) torque

c) compression

> **Vocabulary tip**
>
> Many words in English have more than one meaning. Sometimes, the meanings are connected, for example:
> *impact* (physical) – when one object hits another
> *impact* (figurative) – the effect that something has on someone or something.

VOCABULARY FOR READING — Engineering and technology — Multiple meanings

3a Find words in the text which mean ...

a) (paragraph 1) how something is made: _design_ (noun).

b) (paragraph 1) to hit something repeatedly and hard: ...., ... (verbs).

c) (paragraph 1) devices that can react to light, movement, etc.: .... (noun).

d) (paragraph 1) when one object hits another: .... (noun).

e) (paragraph 2) how serious something is: .... (noun).

f) (paragraph 2) to check how fast, strong, etc. something is: ...., ... (verbs).

g) (paragraph 2) how well something works: .... (noun).

h) (paragraph 3) a company that makes something: .... (noun).

3b Complete the sentences using words from 3a. In some cases, more than one option may be possible.

a) When building flood defences, engineers have to consider the frequency and .... of flooding.

b) The lights are triggered by movement ...., so they come on when someone enters the room.

c) Engineering students look at examples of poor product .... to learn about mistakes to avoid.

d) All the major car .... are now trying to develop affordable, mass-market electric vehicles.

e) Continuous research and testing is carried out to improve the .... of all our products.

f) Special equipment is used to continuously .... levels of pollution in the air around the city.

g) The glass bottle shattered on .... with the wall.

h) The buildings were .... by high winds and heavy rains during the storm causing some damage.

EXAM TASK: Reading (diagram label completion)

4 Which paragraph of the article opposite explains in detail how the crash-test dummies work?

5 Label the diagram below. Choose NO MORE THAN THREE WORDS from the passage for each answer.

Exam tip

Make sure you understand what the diagram shows and what kind of information is needed to fill the gaps. Match the parts of the diagram to information in the text. The information you need will often be in one part of the text.

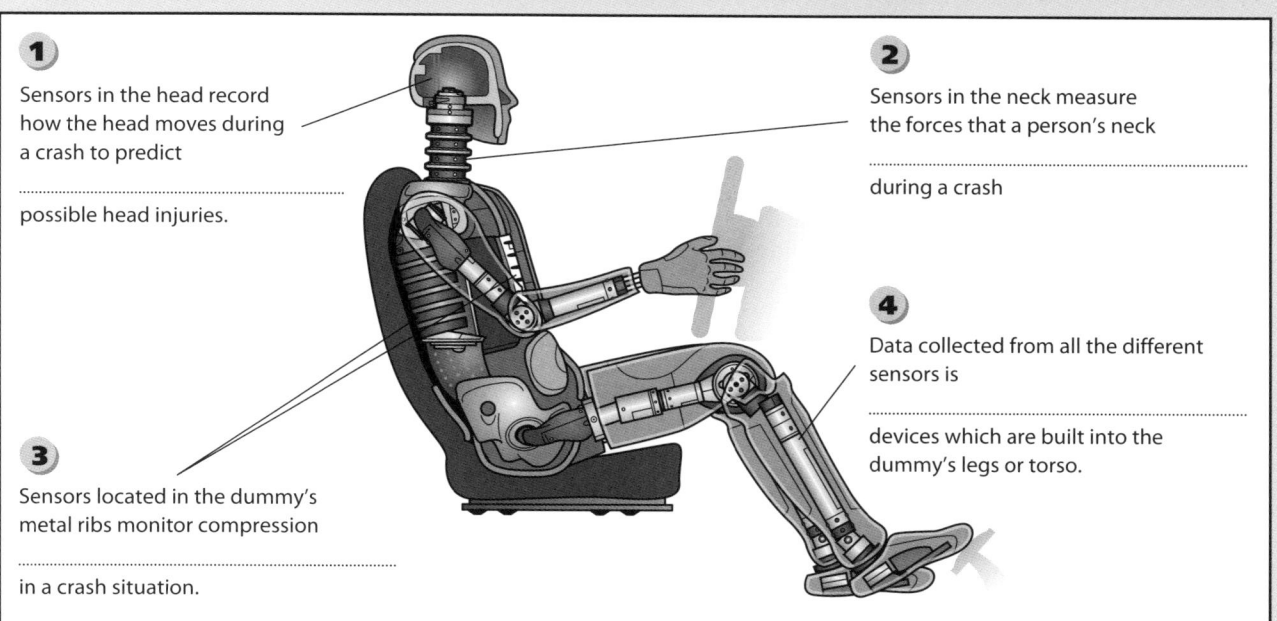

1 Sensors in the head record how the head moves during a crash to predict .... possible head injuries.

2 Sensors in the neck measure the forces that a person's neck .... during a crash

3 Sensors located in the dummy's metal ribs monitor compression .... in a crash situation.

4 Data collected from all the different sensors is .... devices which are built into the dummy's legs or torso.

VOCABULARY FOR READING — Culture and tradition — Synonyms and antonyms

A way of life

1 Work in groups. Read the definition of *nomadic* and discuss the questions.

nomadic (*adj*) (of a group of people) moving often from place to place without one permanent home

- What groups of traditionally nomadic people do you know about? Where do they live?
- Why do they live a nomadic way of life?
- How do you think these traditional lifestyles might be affected in the modern world?

2 Read the first part of the article and answer the questions.

a) Which group of nomadic people does the text mention?
b) Where do they live?
c) Why do they move from place to place?
d) What is threatening their way of life?

Dashing through the snow

An annual reindeer race seeks to keep herding traditions alive in the threatened Arctic

A unique tradition celebrates the arrival of spring in Inari, Lapland, in northern Finland: the Reindeer Cup Championship. Finland's native Sami people hold the reindeer racing event every year. But this tradition, along with the Sami's herding culture, is under threat. The culprit: human impact on the environment.

Finland has 51 reindeer herding co-operatives, many of which take part in the championships. The herders compete to see who owns the strongest and fastest reindeer. During the race, reindeer pull jockeys on skis at speeds of up to 60 kilometres per hour.

Reindeer are an important part of the Sami's livelihoods. Throughout the year, the Sami migrate with their animals across the permanently frozen ground of the Arctic tundra. Reindeer are well adapted to live in this freezing, barren landscape. But climate change, mining, and logging are making it harder for the reindeer to survive in the Arctic and for the Sami to continue living their indigenous way of life.

3a Match the words and phrases with a similar meaning.

1 tradition   a) lifestyle
2 native   b) job
3 livelihood   c) custom
4 way of life   d) indigenous

3b How do the pairs of words in 3a differ in meaning or usage? Use a dictionary to help you if necessary.

4 Complete the statements using words from the text.

a) The traditional Sami herding culture is under .... from a number of sources.
b) Different factors are making it difficult for the reindeer to .... and for the Sami to continue with their traditional way of life.
c) Although environmental factors are having a negative impact, the main .... is human activity.
d) Nevertheless, the Sami are trying hard to .... their traditions alive.

VOCABULARY FOR READING — Culture and tradition — Synonyms and antonyms

5 Read the second part of the article and match the summaries below to the paragraphs they describe.

1 How the reindeer are used ....
2 The threats to reindeer herding ....
3 The history of reindeer as domesticated animals ....
4 Plans to protect reindeer herding ....
5 About the Sami people ....

Raising reindeer

A Reindeer are semi-domesticated cousins of the caribou, found mostly in the Arctic and sub-Arctic. The Dukha, a small nomadic tribe that lives in the remote mountains of Mongolia, are believed to have been the first people to domesticate these animals, more than 3,000 years ago.

B Today, more than 20 indigenous groups in the Arctic practise this type of animal husbandry, or the raising and breeding of domesticated animals. One such group is the Sami who inhabit a wilderness area called Sapmi, which stretches across parts of Norway, Sweden, Finland, and Russia.

C Although a few herding cultures use reindeer for transportation and milk production, most raise them for food. 'Reindeer meat is high in protein and low in fat,' says Greg Finstad, programme manager for the Reindeer Research Programme at the University of Alaska Fairbanks. 'It tends to be healthier than other meat due to the pristine environment in which the animal grazes.'

A threatened tradition

D Today, reindeer husbandry faces many challenges. Climate change has disturbed the fragile environment that reindeer depend on for survival. But human intrusion is a more immediate danger. According to the Association of Reindeer Herding Co-operatives in Finland, logging, power plants, and other forms of land use have taken over reindeer pastures and disrupted their migration patterns. Hundreds of migrating reindeer are killed by automobiles each year. Mining companies compete for land and their methods often contaminate feeding grounds.

E International reindeer herding organisations continue to advocate stronger laws to protect reindeer, their environment, and the herding trade. In spite of the challenges though, the herding culture perseveres.

6 Find words in the article with the opposite meaning of those in bold below.

a) (paragraph A) a **wild** animal _domesticated_
b) (paragraph B) a **built-up, urban** area ....
c) (paragraph C) a **contaminate**d area ....
d) (paragraph D) a **strong** environment ....
e) (paragraph E) to **oppose** an idea ....

✎ EXAM TASK: Reading (short answer questions)

7 Look at the complete article. Write NO MORE THAN THREE WORDS AND / OR A NUMBER from the article for each question.

> **Exam tip**
> For each question, find the section of the text that is about that topic and underline it. The questions will be in the same order as the information in the text.

1 Which community takes part in the reindeer racing championships?
   ....
2 How fast can the reindeer go in the races? ....
3 What area do the Sami move across with their reindeer? ....
4 When were reindeer first thought to have been domesticated? ....
5 How many different groups of native people herd reindeer? ....
6 What do the reindeer herders mostly use the animals for? ....
7 What is the greatest threat to the reindeer? ....
8 What do reindeer herders want in order to protect their way of life? ....

VOCABULARY FOR READING Crime and policing   Verb patterns

Crime fighters

1 Work in groups. Discuss the threats to wildlife below. Check any words in the dictionary if necessary.

> habitat loss   invasive species   poaching   pollution

- How is wildlife threatened by each of these issues?
- Do you know of any specific examples of these threats?
- How does the law deal with these issues?
- What are the challenges for police and other agencies in preventing crimes that affect wildlife?

2a Read the article. Write questions about it using each of the prompts below.

- Who …?
- How …?
- Where …?
- Why …?
- What …?

Wildlife crime fighters

In South Africa, a group of young women protects a nature reserve's animals

As the full moon rises over the Balule Nature Reserve in South Africa, a group of young women are getting ready for patrol. They will spend the night perched in jeeps looking for a break in the fence, a well-hidden snare trap, or any other sign of poachers. Their job is particularly important – and dangerous – under a full moon.

That's when poachers take advantage of the bright light to illegally hunt the park's animals. These women are members of the Black Mamba Anti-Poaching Unit – the world's first all-female squad dedicated to stopping illegal hunting. The goal of the 26-member group is to stop poachers from killing the park's animals, such as endangered rhinos and elephants. Team members work in shifts around the clock. They check vehicles that come through the reserve, guard the border, set up roadblocks, remove poachers' snares, and patrol on foot.

'Poachers have big guns. We have pepper spray and handcuffs, but we are not afraid,' says Leitah Mkhebela. At 22 years old, she is one of the youngest Black Mambas. If they see poachers, the Black Mambas call for armed backup. But their very presence has helped save wildlife.

The rhinoceros is one of the park's most threatened animals. More than 1,000 rhinos were poached in South Africa in 2014 – about one every eight hours. Their horns are prized in other countries, primarily those in Asia. Rhino horn is used in traditional medicine, even though it has no proven medical benefit. In some cases, poachers cut off a rhino's horn and leave the animal to die.

Rhinos are not the only animals under siege. As park rangers have focused efforts on protecting rhinos, elephant poaching has returned to the world-famous Kruger National Park for the first time in more than a decade. The park shares a fenceless border with Balule, so the Black Mambas' work affects animals in both parks.

Since the Black Mambas started patrolling in 2013, they've had many successes protecting the park's animals. The number of rhinos lost to poaching in Balule has plummeted. Nine poachers have been caught, and the number of illegal snares has shrunk dramatically.

The Black Mambas hope their work will ensure rhinos, elephants, and all of the park's other animals are still alive for years to come. 'The next generation must know rhinos and elephants,' says Lukie Mahlake. 'If poaching is allowed, they will only see these animals in a picture.'

2b Swap your questions with a partner. Answer their questions.

VOCABULARY FOR READING | Crime and policing | Verb patterns

3 Find words or phrases in the article which have a similar meaning to the underlined expressions below.

a) Soldiers <u>stand outside</u> the entrance to the palace <u>to stop unauthorized people going in</u>. _guard_

b) Police set up <u>obstacles in the road to stop vehicles passing through without being checked</u> on all main roads out of the city. ....

c) Armed police <u>walk around</u> the airport keeping a lookout for suspicious behaviour. ....

d) Local police called for <u>officers who are trained to use firearms to help them</u> when it became clear that the man had a gun. ....

e) Just <u>the fact that people can see</u> security guards in a store is often enough to deter thieves. ....

f) Many homes in the area have guard dogs <u>to stop</u> the residents <u>being attacked or harmed by intruders</u>.
....

4a Find the expressions in the article and identify the verb form which comes next: *to do* (an infinitive), *doing* (a gerund) or *do* (an infinitive without *to*).

a) take advantage of the bright light to *illegally hunt* – to do
b) dedicated to .... - ....
c) the goal of the 26-member group is .... - ....
d) stop poachers from .... - ....
e) has helped .... - ....
f) have focused efforts on .... - ....

Vocabulary tip

Many words are typically followed by a particular verb form: *dedicated to + -ing*. Some words can be followed by more than one verb form: *start to do / start doing*.

4b Complete the sentences using a form of the verb in CAPITALS. More than one form may be possible.

a) During the summer months, thieves take advantage of homeowners being away on holiday .... unnoticed. BREAK IN

b) CCTV footage can help police .... criminals if the film quality is good enough. IDENTIFY

c) Security tags are designed to stop shoplifters from .... the store with unpaid-for goods. LEAVE

d) The force has a group of officers dedicated to .... with schools and community groups. LIAISE

e) The main goal of this new campaign is .... awareness of human trafficking. RAISE

✏ EXAM TASK: Reading (summary completion)

5 Complete the summary of the article opposite using the list of words below.

Exam tip

Read the full sentence to check that your chosen word works grammatically and that the meaning matches the information in the text.

A dedicated   B focused   C goal   D hunting   E on patrol
F patrol   G poach   H presence   I protect   J success

The Black Mambas are an all-female anti-poaching unit who (1) .... the Balule Nature Reserve in South Africa to (2) .... the wildlife from poachers. The women are not armed themselves, but just their (3) .... in the park has helped stop poachers from illegally (4) .... the endangered animals which live in the reserve. Initially they (5) .... their attention on protecting rhinos. The number of rhinos lost to poachers has dropped dramatically since they started operating, but the ultimate (6) .... of the Black Mambas is to stamp out poaching of all the park's animals.

VOCABULARY FOR READING | Business and finance | Meaning and context

Making music, making money

1 Work in groups. Look at the figures below and discuss the impact that digital music formats are having on musicians.

- What is the difference between retail CD sales, downloads and streaming?
- Which method of distributing music is most profitable for musicians?
- Which method of accessing music do you think is most popular in your country/worldwide?
- How is the way you buy and listen to music different from your parents' generation?

ONLINE MUSIC: A BAD DEAL FOR ARTISTS

The number of sales, downloads or songs plays a solo artist would have to rack up each month to make minimum wage in the U.S.*

Retail CD sales	1,161
iTunes album downloads	1,226
iTunes song downloads	11,364
Song plays on streaming platform Last.fm	849,817
Song plays on streaming platform Spotify	4,053,110

*Based on a U.S. monthly minimum wage of approximately $1,260

2 Read the article. Put the words below into three groups:

a) Things you can hold in your hand   b) Things that only exist in digital form

c) Things that can be both

> albums   cassette tapes   CDs   digital files   downloads
> hard-copy recordings   MP3s   physical formats   platforms
> records   singles   songs   streaming

MUSIC INDUSTRY MAYHEM

Digital downloads have changed the music industry

Before Spotify, before Pandora, before the Internet, you had to go to the store and buy a record to hear your favourite song (if you weren't lucky enough to hear it on the radio that day). Albums only came in physical formats like CDs, cassette tapes, and records.

Not anymore. The Internet has turned the music industry upside down. First came MP3s, digital files you can download and listen to on your computer and iPod. Then Apple opened the iTunes Store in 2003, so a 99-cent single was only a click away.

Unfortunately for the music industry, downloading MP3s meant fewer people bought hard-copy recordings and revenue declined. In 2003, US revenue for the music industry was $12 billion. By 2013, it had shrunk to about $7 billion, according to the Recording Industry Association of America.

Yet during that time, revenue from digital music downloads has skyrocketed – starting from zero in 2003 to about $4.5 billion in 2013. Pirated music has also soared during this time.

Today, streaming websites like Pandora and Spotify let you listen to just about any song you want. But these free or nearly free websites make it hard for musicians to earn a living.

To save their profession, some artists have fought back. Taylor Swift removed her music from Spotify in November 2014. And Irish rock band U2 is working to create an entirely new digital music format that can't be pirated. They hope that these changes will help all musicians earn more.

* **pirate** (verb) to illegally make copies of software, music, films, books, etc., usually to sell

3a Find two words in the text which describe ...

a) an upward trend.   b) a downward trend.

3b What helped you to work out the meaning of the words?

Vocabulary tip

The context that a word appears in can help you to guess the meaning.
revenue was $12 billion ... by 2013, it had **shrunk** to $7 billion (shrunk = downward trend)
revenue has **skyrocketed** - starting from zero ... to 4.5 billion (skyrocketed = upward trend)

VOCABULARY FOR READING   Businesss and finance   Meaning and context

3c **Do the bold words describe an upward or a downward trend? Use the context to work out the meaning.**

a) The popular talent show seemed to have hit **a slump**. Because of last season's lower ratings, the show's creators are hoping to attract new viewers with new judges.

b) Where previously there were hundreds of jobs listed on the site, in recent times it has **dwindled** to less than a couple of dozen.

c) Business confidence in the economy has **rallied** strongly in the March quarter, increasing to levels not experienced since 2008.

d) The average home price **tumbled** 29 percent to an eight-year low of $164,600 in February.

e) Then fuel prices **went through the roof** last year and I had to look for ways to cut our bills.

f) Smartphone sales **surpassed** 40 million units, a 27 per cent increase from the same period last year.

4 **Choose the most appropriate word or phrase to complete the sentences.**

a) Apparently free websites are able to make *a living / profit* by selling advertising space.

b) The average *revenue / salary* of a secondary school teacher is around €28,000.

c) The company employs workers who are paid a *living / the minimum wage* and receive no benefits.

d) Does the local community benefit from the *salary / revenue* generated by tourism or does it just go to the owners of a few luxury hotels?

e) For some families, rent accounts for more than 40% of their household *income / wages*.

f) Most people don't make *income / money* from blogging, but it is a good way to raise your profile.

EXAM TASK: Reading (multiple selection)

5 **Choose THREE letters, A–G. According to the article opposite, which THREE of the following were true in 2003?**

A Consumers could either listen to music on the radio or buy recordings from a shop.

B People started downloading music to listen to on their computer or other device.

C Consumers could download an album for less than one dollar.

D The revenue from the music industry in the US was around $12 billion.

E Revenue from downloaded music was approximately $4.5 billion.

F Music piracy was a big problem for the music industry and artists.

G It was not yet possible to stream music for free from the internet.

6 **Choose THREE letters, A–G. According to the article, which THREE of the following trends were seen between 2003 and 2013?**

A Money earned from the sale of hard-copy recordings of music dropped.

B The number of people buying music overall in the US fell.

C The cost of downloading digital recordings of music went down.

D In general, music industry profits worldwide rose steadily.

E Income from digital downloads grew dramatically.

F The amount of music being copied and sold illegally increased.

G Musicians made significantly more money from downloads and streaming.

Exam tip

Read the instructions carefully. For multiple choice questions, you are asked to choose one correct answer.
For multiple selection questions, you are asked to choose several correct answers.

VOCABULARY FOR WRITING: TASK 1 — Describing graphs, charts and diagrams

Figure it out!

1 Work in pairs. Look at the five figures.

1 Match the words in the box to the five figures below.
2 What is the general topic of each set of data?
3 Are any of the data sets connected to each other?
4 Which topic do you find the most interesting?

> bar chart   diagram   graph   pie chart   table

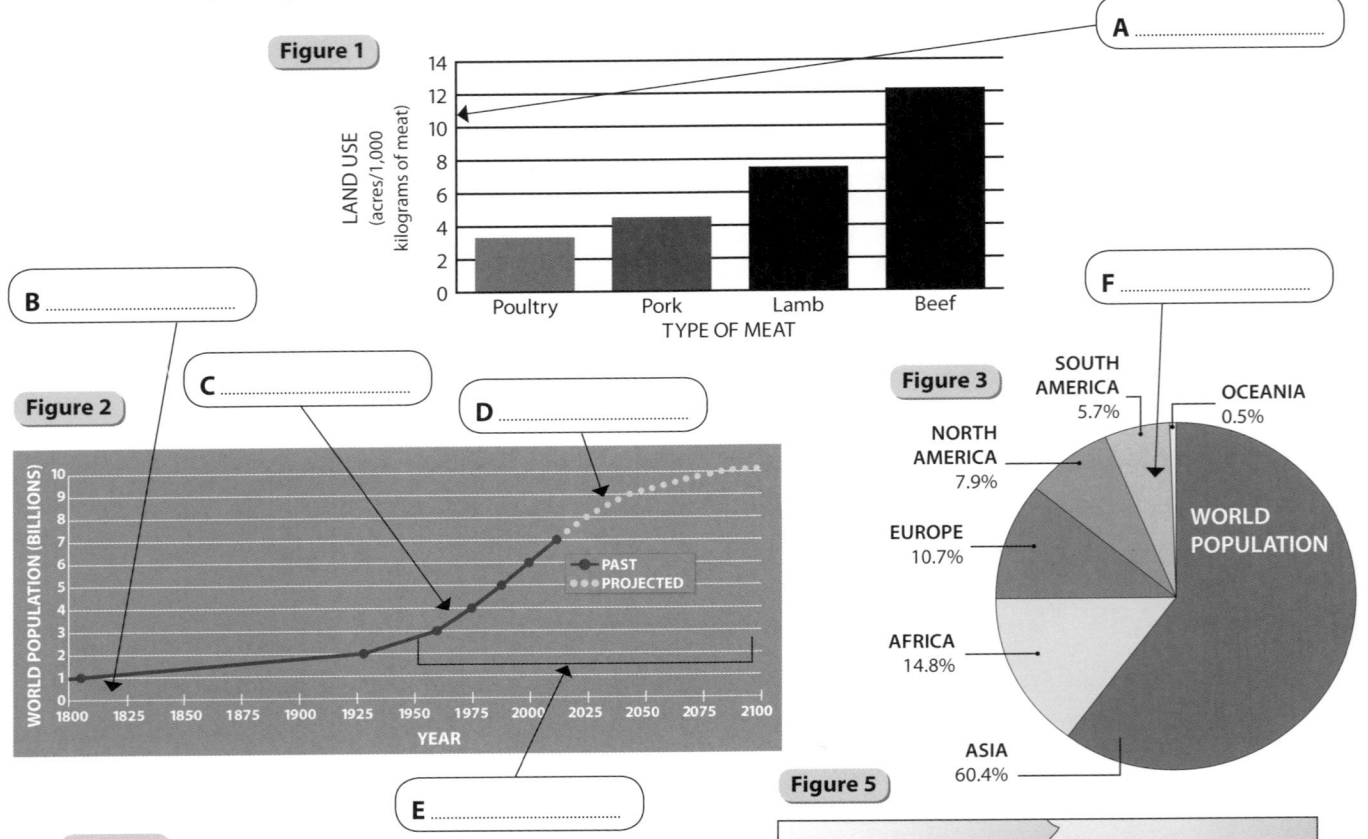

Figure 4

Average life expectancy (in years)

Country	Men	Women
Australia	80	84
Brazil	71	78
China	74	77
India	67	69
Japan	81	87
Russia	65	76
South Africa	55	59
UK	79	83

Source of data: World Bank

2 Complete labels A–H on figures 1–5 using words from the box.

> column   curve   dotted line   horizontal axis
> row   segment   solid line   vertical axis

Vocabulary tip

Figure can be used as a general word to describe any kind of graph, chart or diagram: *The first figure shows …, In Figure 1, … .* Figures are also numbers, especially in the form of statistics: *The figures for life expectancy … .*

VOCABULARY FOR WRITING: TASK 1 — Describing graphs, charts and diagrams

3 Match the sentence halves. Think about both the overall meaning and the function of the highlighted verb.

1. A pie chart **shows**
2. The size of each segment in a pie chart **represents**
3. Arrows on a diagram typically **indicate**
4. A diagram might **illustrate**
5. The height of each bar in a bar chart **corresponds to**
6. The graph here **shows**

a) a process or the structure of something.
b) different quantities as a proportion of a total.
c) a number on the vertical axis.
d) the sequence of different stages or events in a process.
e) the rapid increase in the world's population.
f) a certain proportion, usually expressed as a percentage.

4a Work in pairs. Write sentences describing the figures using the sentence beginnings in A and the verbs in B. Use each verb at least once.

Example: *The bar chart illustrates the amount of land needed to produce different types of meat.*

A
The bar chart
The pie chart
The table)
The diagram
Each of the bars in the chart
The vertical axis of the graph
The dotted line in the graph
The largest segment of the pie chart
Each numbered part of the diagram
The figures in the third column

B
show
represent
correspond to
indicate
illustrate

4b In pairs, write at least 4 more sentences describing different features of the figures.

5 In pairs, choose one of the figures and identify 2 or 3 of the most interesting or significant points in the data. When you look at the data, what jumps out first?

Example: *The pie chart shows that by far the largest proportion of the world's population lives in Asia.*

Exam tip

A data commentary typically includes:
Introduction: one sentence introducing the topic
Overview: one or two sentences picking out the most significant points
Expansion: two or three sentences giving more details about these points.

✏ EXAM TASK: Writing (Task 1)

6 Choose one of the figures 1–4 and write a paragraph describing it. Write at least 150 words. Include:

- an introduction: one sentence introducing the overall topic
- an overview: one or two sentences identifying the most interesting or significant features of the data
- some expansion: more detail about what the data shows – here you can include details of the significant features such as specific numbers.

Exam tip

You don't need to describe every feature of the graph or chart. You should pick out only the most significant features to describe.

VOCABULARY FOR WRITING: TASK 1 — Expressing numbers and statistics

Pick a number

1a Work in pairs or small groups. Read the text and match the numbers to the facts. You'll need to make some guesses!

5.2   80   450   547   1630   1,933   3,600   8,740,000   250,000,000

a) .... species live on Earth, according to recent estimates. About 85 percent of these species have yet to be discovered!

b) .... percent of 11-to 20-year-olds underestimate the number of calories in fast foods – often by hundreds of calories.

c) .... hectares is the area one animal covered in a study that tracked housecats' movements for two years.

d) $............... is the price a 104-year-old biscuit sold for at auction. Explorer Ernest Shackleton took the biscuit on one of his famous expeditions to the Antarctic.

e) .... feet to 6.3 feet, that's 1.58 to 1.92 metres, is the height requirement for NASA astronauts.

f) .... cases of malaria occur every year. A new vaccine against the mosquito-borne illness cut the rate of infection in children by 56 percent.

g) .... is the year Rembrandt painted Bearded Old Man. Scientists now know the Dutch artist painted the picture, as X-rays revealed his self-portrait underneath.

h) .... kilograms is about the weight of a huge fungus found in China. It's the largest ever documented.

i) .... metres underground is the depth at which the deepest-living animal – a 0.5-millimetre-long worm – has been found.

1b Explain your choices to the class. Be careful about how you pronounce the numbers!

2 Quick quiz! Work in pairs. Take turns to ask and answer about the text above using the prompts below. Answer as quickly – but as accurately! – as possible.

How long …?   How far …?
How old …?   How deep …?
How many …?   How heavy …?
How tall …?   What percentage of …?

> **Vocabulary tip**
>
> When a phrase including a number (such as age, size, etc.) comes before the noun it describes, it is hyphenated:
> *a 104-year-old biscuit, a 0.5-millimetre-long worm.*
>
> When the phrase comes after a verb, it doesn't have hyphens:
> *The biscuit was 104 years old.*
> *The worm is just 0.5 millimetres long.*

3 Reword the expressions. Pay special attention to the hyphens.

a) a 104-year-old biscuit – *a biscuit that was 104 years old*

b) 11- to 20-year-olds – ....

c) a study that lasted for two years – ....

d) an area of 547 hectares – ....

e) a mosquito-borne illness – ....

f) a fungus weighing 420 kilograms – ....

VOCABULARY FOR WRITING: TASK 1 — Expressing numbers and statistics

4a Complete the explanations using the words from the box.

> amount   estimate   majority   maximum   minimum   number   percentage   period   range   rate

a) The *majority* is the largest part of something, always more than 50%.

b) A(n) .... is a part of something expressed as if the whole is equal to 100.

c) If a number can .... between x and y, then those are the lower and upper limits.

d) A(n) .... is a quantity of something that is viewed as uncountable: water, air, land, etc.

e) A(n) .... is a quantity of something that is viewed as countable: people, cars, animals, etc.

f) The .... at which something happens is the speed over time: 6 per hour, 100 per day, etc.

g) If you .... something, you make a guess based on evidence.

h) The .... is the largest possible quantity, size, speed, etc.

i) The .... is the smallest possible quantity, size, speed, etc.

j) A .... is a length of time: 5 minutes, 24 hours, 5 days, etc.

4b Complete the statements about the text opposite using words from exercise 4a. More than one option may be possible.

a) Scientists have *estimated* that there are almost 9 million species on Earth.

b) A very large .... of those species haven't yet been discovered.

c) The .... of teenagers underestimate the .... of calories in fast foods.

d) One study measured the .... of land that pet cats covered over a .... of two years.

e) The height of a NASA astronaut can .... between 1.58 and 1.92 metres.

f) The new malaria vaccine reduced the .... of infection by over half.

g) 3,600 metres underground is the .... depth that living creatures have been found.

5 Work in pairs. Read the text in the box about the world's population. Write sentences about the information using some of the phrases below.

Example: *65 percent of the world's population range between 15 and 65 years old.*

the percentage / majority of ... range between ... and ...

only a small minority of ...

a substantial number / proportion of ...

just over / under half of ...

WHO ARE THE 7 BILLION?

If 100 peope were chosen to represent the diversity of humans on the planet, they would have the following demographics. (These numbers translate into percentages that can be applied to the enitire population.)

GENDER - 51 men, 49 women

RELIGION - 33 Christians, 22 Muslims, 14 Hindu, 7 Buddhist, 12 other, 12 non-religious

NATIVE LANGUAGE - 12 Mandarin Chinese, 5 English, 5 Spanish, 3 Arabic, 3 Hindi, 72 other

AGE - 27 are younger than 15, 65 are between ages 15 and 65, 8 are older than 65

EDUCATION - 16 can't read or write, 35 have internet access

LOCALE - 51 live in cities, 49 live in rural areas

✎ EXAM TASK: Writing (Task 1)

6 Write a paragraph describing the text in the box. Include:

- an introductory sentence explaining the topic
- at least one sentence about each section
- language to link your ideas together.

Exam tip

Remember not to use abbreviations in the exam. Write measurements in words: *450 kilograms* (NOT *450kg*), *1.58 metres* (NOT *1.58m*).

VOCABULARY FOR WRITING: TASK 1 — Describing trends

Trending

1a Work in pairs or small groups. Read the information about the three graphs and discuss your answers to the questions below.

Maine Concern

For decades, the US state of Maine has kept records of the seafood caught off its coasts. Scientists and government officials use this data to create fishing guidelines for a variety of species. When comparing long-term data like this, you should look for the following:

- upward trend: data sets that show an overall increase over time
- downward trend: data sets that show an overall decrease over time
- no trend: data sets that show no clear trend
- outlier: a data point that lies far outside the overall distribution of the data set.

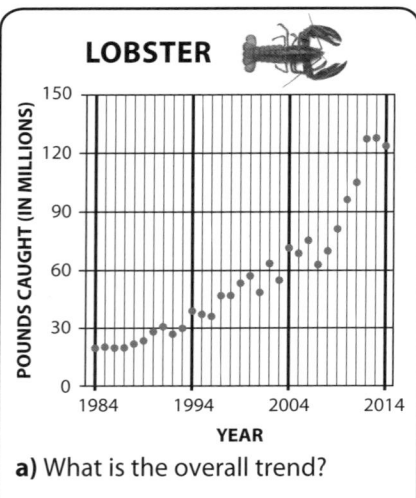

a) What is the overall trend?

b) Are there outliers in the data? If so, in which year(s)?

c) Look at the years 1984, 1994, 2004 and 2014. During which 10-year period did the lobster harvest experience the most growth?

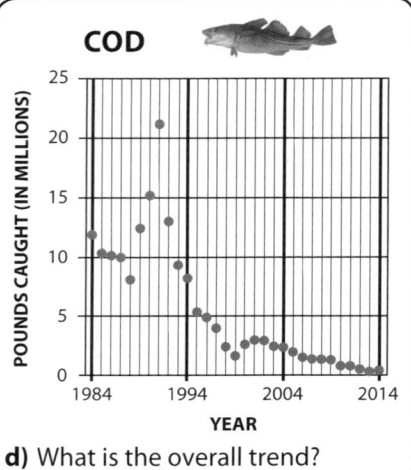

d) What is the overall trend?

e) Are there outliers in the data? If so, in which year(s)?

f) What is the overall trend in the amount of cod harvested between 2004 and 2013?

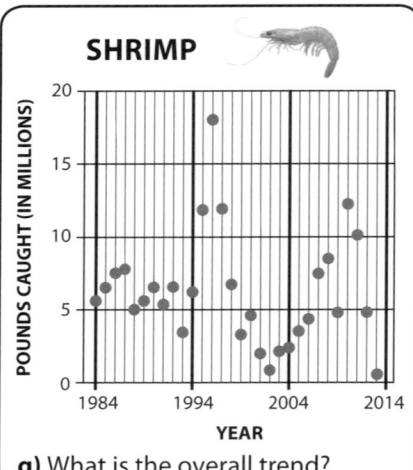

g) What is the overall trend?

h) Are there outliers in the data? If so, in which year(s)?

i) What word(s) might describe the trend in this graph? What type of factors might account for this pattern?

1b Compare your answers with other groups/pairs. Did you agree on all the answers?

2 Read a student's description of the first graph and complete it using words from the box. Some words are not needed.

> growth   number   peak   quantity   raised   reaching   rose   steadily   touching   trend   upward

The first graph shows the **(a)** .... of lobster caught off the coast of Maine over the period from 1984 to 2004. The overall **(b)** .... is **(c)** .... starting at less than 30 million pounds in 1984 and **(d)** .... a **(e)** .... of over 120 million pounds per year by 2014. The amount of lobster caught **(f)** .... **(g)** .... over the period, with the most dramatic **(h)** .... occurring between 2004 and 2014.

VOCABULARY FOR WRITING: TASK 1 — Describing trends

3a Label the words in the box as verbs (v) or adverbs (adv) …

> decline (*v*)   dramatically (*adv*)   drastically (…)   expand (…)   fall (…)   fast (…)   gradually (…)
> grow (…)   improve (…)   reduce (…)   rise (…)   sharply (…)   shrink (…)   steadily (…)

3b Which verbs and adverbs …
- describe a movement upwards?
- describe a movement downwards?
- express a slow change?
- express a large or sudden change?

3c Which of the verbs in exercise 3a are usually transitive (like *raise*), which are usually intransitive (like *rise*) and which can be both?

4a Rewrite the sentences replacing the highlighted verb with a noun or the highlighted noun with a verb. Make any other changes necessary.

a) Each employee's workload has **expanded** dramatically.

Each employee has experienced a dramatic expansion in their workload.

b) There has been a gradual **decline** in the number of local cinemas.

c) The company is **growing** fast in Asia.

d) The new design will drastically **reduce** energy costs.

e) The number of flu cases **rises** sharply in the winter months.

f) The school has seen a steady **improvement** in students' average exam grades.

4b Work with a partner. How many different ways can you think of to describe these trends?

Example: *a gradual rise (b), a dramatic reduction (c).*

Vocabulary tip

Rise is an intransitive verb – something rises. It is not followed by an object and it cannot be passive.
Prices **have risen** by 10%.
Raise is a transitive verb – someone raises something. It is usually followed by an object.
The government **raised taxes**.

Exam tip

You can make your writing more interesting, and show a greater range of vocabulary, by using a mix of different word forms to describe trends.
verb + adverb: *rise steadily, grow dramatically*
adjective + noun: *a steady rise, dramatic growth*

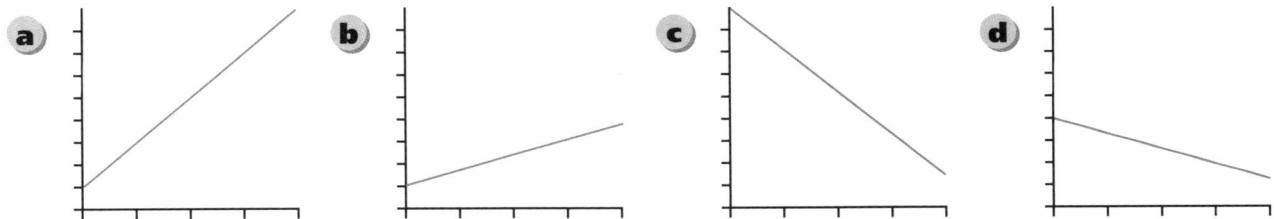

✎ EXAM TASK

5a Work in pairs. Discuss how you could describe the trends shown in the graphs for cod and shrimp. Choose which points to highlight.

5b Choose one graph each and, individually, write a draft paragraph. Write 3–4 sentences.

5c Share your paragraph with your partner. Work together to make any corrections or improvements. Think about these questions.
- Does the text include a range of different vocabulary to describe the trend?
- Have you used a mix of different word forms (verb + adverb, adjective + noun)?
- Have you used appropriate prepositions where necessary?

VOCABULARY FOR WRITING: TASK 1 — Making comparisons

The same but different

1 Work in groups. Read the short text about World Heritage Sites and discuss the questions.

What's a World Heritage Site?
United Nations World Heritage Sites are cultural and natural places that are deemed to have "outstanding universal value". A site could be an important piece of human history, an architectural marvel, or an area of exceptional natural beauty.

Abu Simbel temples, Egypt

1 Do you know any World Heritage Sites in your country? Have you ever visited a World Heritage site?

2 What type of places might be World Heritage Sites because of their historical or architectural importance or because of their natural beauty?

3 What type of threats do you think might put World Heritage Sites in danger? How can they be protected?

2a Look at the information in the table below. Work in groups to answer the questions.

a) Which region has the largest number of heritage sites? What percentage of the total does this represent?

b) What type of World Heritage Site makes up the largest part of the total?

c) What proportion of the sites in Europe and North America are sites of natural beauty?

d) What percentage of Africa's sites are in danger?

e) In which region are the largest percentage of sites in danger?

HERITAGE SITES BY REGION AND TYPE AS OF 2015

Region	Cultural	Natural	Mixed	Total	In Danger
Africa	48	37	4	89	16
Arab States	73	4	2	79	16
Asia and the Pacific	168	59	11	238*	4
Europe and North America	420	61	10	491*	5
Latin America and the Caribbean	93	36	5	134	7
Total	802	197	32	1,031	48

2b Match these sentence halves from a piece of student writing comparing the data in the table.

1 By far the greatest number of World Heritage sites are in Europe and North America, …

2 In contrast, Africa and the Arab States have the smallest number of sites, …

3 Overall, the majority of sites, 802, are of cultural interest compared with …

4 In Europe and North America around 85% of sites are of cultural interest as opposed to …

5 In Africa, however, the gap between the number of cultural and natural sites …

6 Whilst there are an equivalent number of sites in danger in Africa and the Arab States, 16 each, …

a) representing around 8% and 7% of the total, respectively.

b) is much smaller.

c) making up approximately 47% of the total.

d) the sites under threat in the Arab States represent a larger proportion of the total sites in that region, roughly 20%.

e) only around 13% which are of natural significance.

f) only 197 sites of natural beauty.

2c Underline words and phrases in exercise 2b that …

- express a comparison.
- describe figures which are not exact.
- describe things which are different / the same.

TIMESAVER FOR EXAMS: IELTS Vocabulary (5.5–7.5) © Scholastic Ltd.

PHOTOCOPIABLE

VOCABULARY FOR WRITING: TASK 1 — Making comparisons

3 Rewrite the sentences using the word or phrase in CAPITALS.

a) August is much more popular than any other month for visitors. BY FAR

August is by far the most popular month for visitors.

b) In comparison with the rest of Spain, the northern coast has relatively high levels of rainfall. COMPARED

c) The first two soft drinks contain exactly the same amount of sugar. EQUIVALENT

d) The drinks labelled as 'light' contain only 5 grams of sugar per 100 grams whereas the standard drinks contain 11 grams. OPPOSED

e) The numbers of boys and girls participating in sport still differ significantly. GAP

f) In urban areas, about 95% of households have access to high-speed broadband. APPROXIMATELY

g) The opposite is true in rural areas where as few as 53% of homes have fast internet connections. CONTRAST

h) The red group and the blue group scored the highest overall; the red group scored an average of 76% and the blue group scored an average of 81%. RESPECTIVELY

4 Work in pairs. Look at the graph showing the distance travelled over a 24-hour period by two coyotes. Answer the questions.

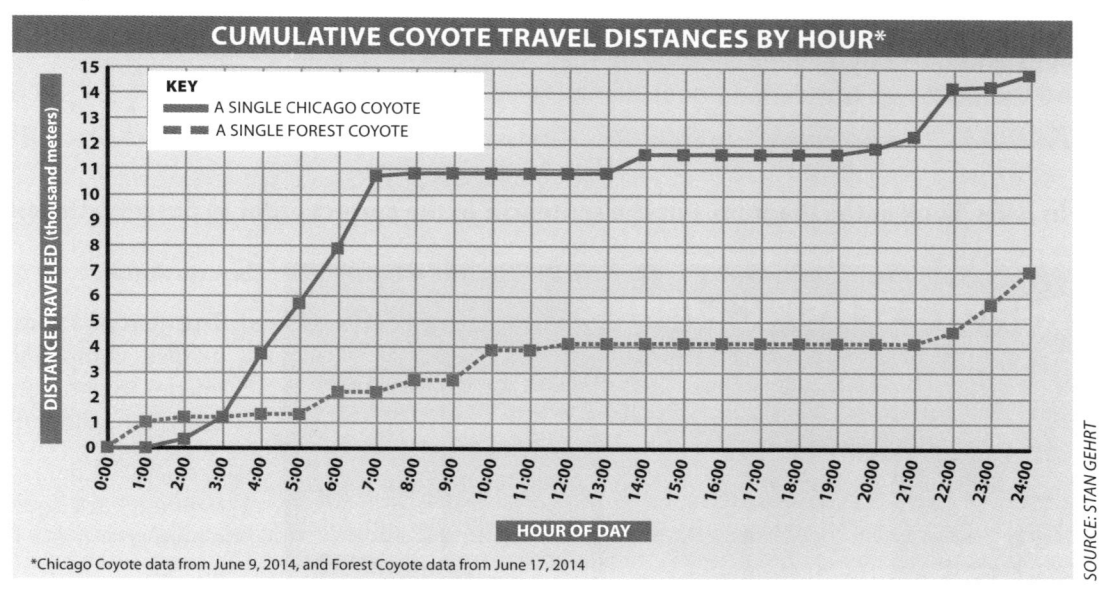

CUMULATIVE COYOTE TRAVEL DISTANCES BY HOUR*

KEY
— A SINGLE CHICAGO COYOTE
- - A SINGLE FOREST COYOTE

DISTANCE TRAVELED (thousand meters) / HOUR OF DAY

*Chicago Coyote data from June 9, 2014, and Forest Coyote data from June 17, 2014

SOURCE: STAN GEHRT

a) Which animal travelled the greatest distance overall in 24 hours?

b) When were the two animals the most active?

c) Around what time had the two coyotes travelled the same distance?

d) By midday, roughly how many more metres had the Chicago coyote travelled than the forest coyote?

e) Both animals travelled very little through the middle part of the day – why do you think this is?

f) Why do you think the coyote living in an urban area travels further overall than its rural counterpart?

EXAM TASK: Writing (Task 1)

5 Summarise the information in the graph by selecting and reporting the main features, and make comparisons where relevant. Write approximately 150 words.

Exam tip

Spend some time looking at all the data and thinking about what it shows before you start writing.

VOCABULARY FOR WRITING: TASK 1 — Describing a process

What comes next?

1a Work in groups. What do you think 'space archaeology' is?

A Sending archaeologists into space to uncover evidence of life on other planets.

B Using archaeological methods to learn more about objects, such as meteorites, that have landed on Earth.

C Using space technology to investigate new archaeological sites in Earth.

1b Read the text to find out whether your ideas were correct.

Space archaeology

Satellites orbiting Earth gather images and data from a distance, a technique called remote sensing. Remote-sensing satellites take pictures of light and other forms of energy reflected and emitted by Earth.

Satellite images allow scientists to see the visual, infrared and thermal parts of the electromagnetic spectrum at the same time. Each type of soil, plant, and mineral reflects and/or emits energy in a unique wavelength, which satellites can detect. Trained archaeologists can look at satellite images and pick out ancient features by their shapes and colours, even when the buildings are buried under plants, sand, and modern buildings.

2a Work in pairs. Look at the diagram. Put the sentences in the correct order to describe the diagram.

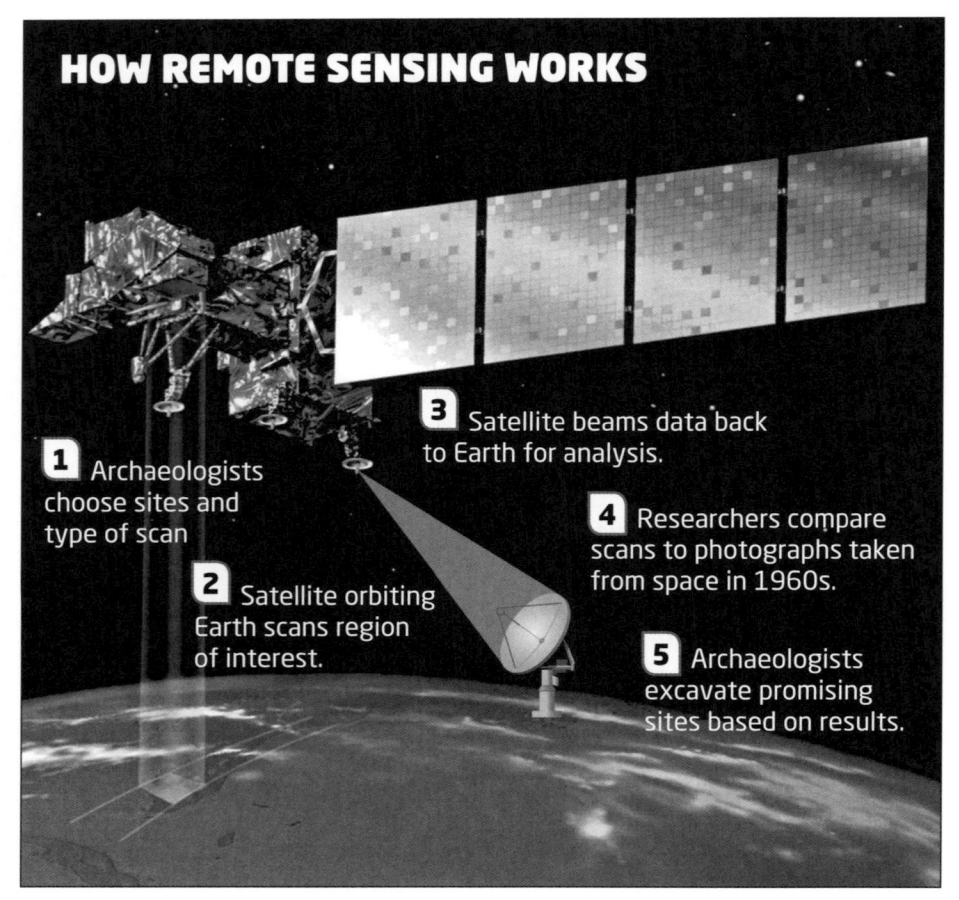

HOW REMOTE SENSING WORKS

1. Archaeologists choose sites and type of scan
2. Satellite orbiting Earth scans region of interest.
3. Satellite beams data back to Earth for analysis.
4. Researchers compare scans to photographs taken from space in 1960s.
5. Archaeologists excavate promising sites based on results.

Description A

a) **The next phase of** the analysis involves comparing the new images to photographs taken in the 1960s to identify changes.

b) The satellite data is then beamed back down to Earth where scientists can analyze the images.

c) The results of the analysis can be used to identify potentially promising sites, but **ultimately** it is archaeologists on the ground who have to excavate the site by hand.

d) **Before** remote sensing can start, archaeologists carry out **preliminary** research to decide what type of scan will be most appropriate for a particular site.

e) During **the first stage of the process**, a satellite orbiting the Earth scans the region of interest.

VOCABULARY FOR WRITING: TASK 1 — Describing a process

Description B

a) Differences between the older and more recent images can reveal changes that might be of interest to archaeologists.

b) The type of scan used is decided prior to the start of this process by archaeologists on the ground.

c) What's more, because the new images can see below the surface features, sites which had initially seemed to be just a mass of vegetation are sometimes shown to contain previously unknown ruins.

d) During remote sensing, satellites, which are continuously orbiting the Earth, are used to scan areas of interest to archaeologists.

e) **Following** the scans, the data is beamed back to Earth for analysis by scientists.

f) The new scans are then compared to images taken by NASA missions some 50 years ago.

2b Compare the two descriptions.
Look out for differences between:

- the order of the information
- the language used to describe sequence
- the features each text describes.

> **Exam tip**
>
> It is not always necessary to describe the stages in a process in exactly the order they appear in a diagram. However, the sequence of the stages must be clear in your description.

3 In each of the sentences in 2a, does the word or phrase in bold indicate that something happens *before* (B) or *after* (A) something else?

✎ EXAM TASK: Writing (Task 1)

4 The diagram shows how special equipment helps new coral to grow in the ocean. Write a report for a university lecturer describing the process. You should write at least 150 words.

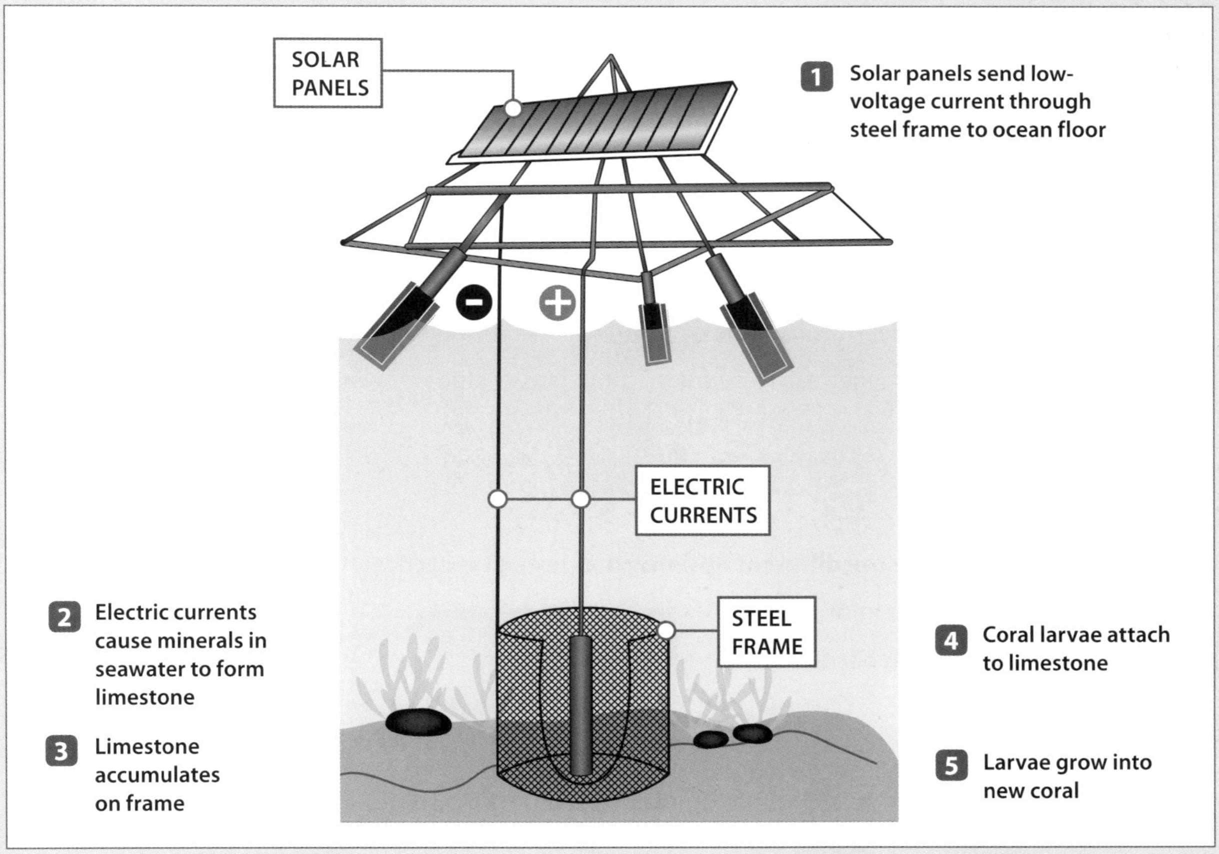

- SOLAR PANELS
- **1** Solar panels send low-voltage current through steel frame to ocean floor
- ELECTRIC CURRENTS
- STEEL FRAME
- **2** Electric currents cause minerals in seawater to form limestone
- **3** Limestone accumulates on frame
- **4** Coral larvae attach to limestone
- **5** Larvae grow into new coral

VOCABULARY FOR WRITING: TASK 1 — Expanding on and rewording labels

In your own words

1a Look at Figures 1 and 2. Ignoring the gaps, match the sentences to the figure they describe.

Figure 1

UK UNIVERSITY GRADUATES IN STEM SUBJECTS 2016

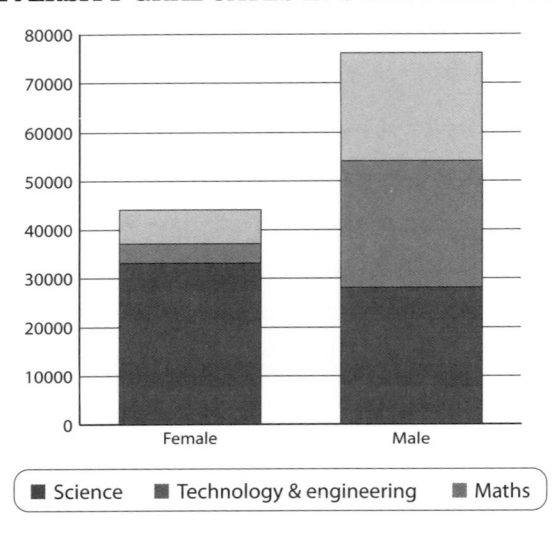

(Bar chart showing Female and Male graduates, with segments for Science, Technology & engineering, and Maths.)

Figure 2

CAREERS OF MATHS GRADUATES

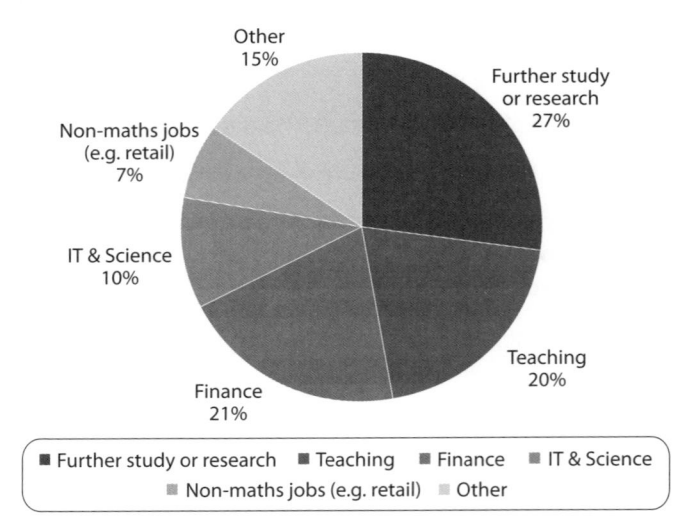

- Further study or research 27%
- Teaching 20%
- Finance 21%
- IT & Science 10%
- Non-maths jobs (e.g. retail) 7%
- Other 15%

a) Around 10% of maths graduates .... in technology or science-related areas.

b) According to the data, significantly more men .... STEM subjects overall than women.

c) A much larger proportion of female students .... science subjects compared with men who .... engineering and maths.

d) Amongst those who leave academia, the most popular career choice for maths graduates is the financial services sector, closely followed by those who .... in education.

Exam tip

Remember that labels on graphs and charts are often in note form. Think about exactly who or what the labels refer to and choose appropriate phrases to talk about them. For example, *female* on a graph could refer to *women* or *girls*, to *female students, female graduates, female employees, female members of staff*, etc.

1b Work in pairs. Complete the sentences in 1a using words and phrases from the box. Add any other words needed. Try to think of several options for each sentence.

> choose   complete/take a course   employ   find work/a job   follow/pursue a career
> get/earn a degree   graduate   study   work

Example: *Around 10% of maths graduates find work /pursue careers/are employed in information technology or science-related areas.*

1c In your pairs, discuss how the different options change each sentence.
- Are they more formal or informal?
- Do they change the emphasis?

Vocabulary tip

Many nouns can be used with – or collocate with – more than one verb. More formal verbs with a specific meaning are appropriate in writing. Try to use a range of verbs in your writing to make it more interesting and to demonstrate your range of vocabulary.

VOCABULARY FOR WRITING: TASK 1 — Expanding on and rewording labels

2a Write verbs from the box which collocate with the key nouns. Some can be used more than once.

> access   buy   browse   download   earn   launch   listen to   make
> market   purchase   raise   receive   search   sell   stream   use

a) the internet ....

b) music ....

c) a product ....
....

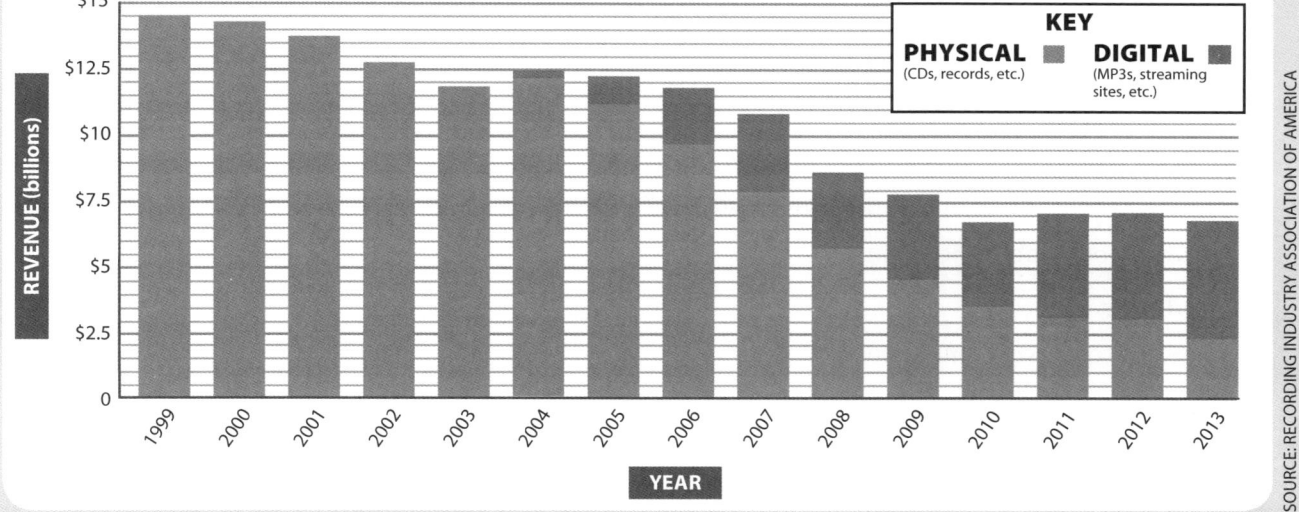

d) money ....

2b Complete the sentences with an appropriate verb. Choose a more formal verb with a specific meaning where possible.

a) In 2017, the company .... several new products aimed specifically at the teenage market.

b) 45% of the people surveyed said that they .... music onto their mobile phone.

c) Only 10% of the people questioned still .... music in physical formats such as CDs.

d) People aged under 25 are more likely to .... the internet for health-related information.

e) As well as income from music sales, musicians also .... money from sales of merchandise and from live concerts.

f) Those in the over 65 age group are the least likely to .... the internet via a mobile device.

g) Over 70 percent of customers prefer to .... high-value products in store rather than online.

h) Many small start-ups now .... money via crowdfunding to get their businesses off the ground.

EXAM TASK: Writing (Task 1)

3 Summarise the information in the graph below by selecting and reporting the main features, and make comparisons where relevant. Write approximately 150 words.

U.S. MUSIC INDUSTRY REVENUE BY FORMAT, 1999-2013

KEY: PHYSICAL (CDs, records, etc.) | DIGITAL (MP3s, streaming sites, etc.)

REVENUE (billions) — $0, $2.5, $5, $7.5, $10, $12.5, $15

YEAR: 1999, 2000, 2001, 2002, 2003, 2004, 2005, 2006, 2007, 2008, 2009, 2010, 2011, 2012, 2013

SOURCE: RECORDING INDUSTRY ASSOCIATION OF AMERICA

VOCABULARY FOR WRITING: TASK 2 — Describing people and groups

Who's who?

1a Write down the names of three people you know.

1b Work in pairs. Ask your partner questions to find out about the three people.

Example: *'How long have you been friends?'*
'Where do you know her from?'

2a Work in groups. Read the extracts from four student essays.

1 Match the bold words to the categories below.

   a) Work & career   b) Family   c) Society

2 Are there any words which don't fit into one of these categories?

A

The school is in a very ethnically diverse area of the city. The **local residents** come from a wide range of different **ethnic groups**. Some of them are recent **migrants**, others are part of more established **communities**.

B

The **staff** at the legal centre are all **experts** in their fields. **Members of the public** can make appointments to get free advice from a qualified legal **professional** on a whole range of issues from **consumer** rights to disputes with **neighbours**.

C

Many people in this **age group** with health problems or disabilities rely on their **spouse** or **partner** as their main carer. It is only where an **individual** has no **relatives** nearby that healthcare **workers** will come in to look after them.

D

The level of motivation within a company's **workforce** is largely dependent on relations between the **employer** and **employees**.

2b Which of the bold words in exercise 2a refer to *individuals* and which refer to *groups*?

3a In groups, take turns to talk about people you know from …

- your work or school/college life.
- your family.
- your social group or community.

Example: *'I have quite a large extended family. My father has five siblings – two brothers and three sisters, so I have lots of relatives.'*

Vocabulary tip

Staff is a group noun – that is, it refers to all the people who work somewhere rather than individual employees. We don't say *a staff* or *staffs*. You can say *a member of staff*.

3b Add any new words for people or groups that came out of your descriptions to the list above.

VOCABULARY FOR WRITING: TASK 2 — Describing people and groups

4a In essays, we often talk about people in general. Choose the best words from the box to complete the statements.

> ~~average~~   everyday   general   stereotypes   traditionally   typical

a) The *average* teenager is probably more interested in sports stars and celebrities than political figures.

b) Sportspeople are often thrust into the media spotlight at a young age so it's not really surprising when they behave like a .... twenty-something.

c) Images that young people see in the media tend to reinforce racial, social and gender ....

d) In many societies, the elderly have .... been looked after within the family, but in a modern world where more women go out to work, caring responsibilities can be difficult to juggle.

e) The .... public tends to have a rather negative view of people beyond retirement age as unproductive and a burden on society.

f) Volunteers can offer older people help with .... tasks such as shopping and cleaning, as well as providing company and contact with people beyond their immediate family.

4b Work in pairs. Do you agree or disagree with the statements in exercise 4a? Explain why.

5a Read the two essay questions below. Match the statements in exercise 4a to the two questions.

> **Exam tip**
>
> When you're writing about people or groups in an essay, think about the best way to describe them. Instead of writing *people*, can you say *consumers*, *professionals*, *local residents* or *members of the public*?

1

Professional sport attracts millions of fans worldwide. Professional sportspeople earn very high salaries and attract massive public attention. It is important therefore that they should act as positive role models for those who follow them.

To what extent do you agree or disagree?

2

Many countries have a growing older population; in Italy 22% of the population are over 65 and in Japan the figure is 26%. In order to look after people who are living much longer, their families will have to find ways to take more responsibility for their care.

To what extent do you agree or disagree?

5b Work in groups. Brainstorm vocabulary that you might use in these essays to refer to individuals and groups.

- Start with words and phrases from the statements in exercise 4 and also from the essay questions themselves.
- Add any more words or phrases that you think might be relevant.

   a) Sporting role models   b) Families and an aging population

5c In groups, list possible arguments agreeing and disagreeing with each of the statements in the questions.

✎ EXAM TASK: Writing (Task 2)

6 Choose one of the essay questions. Write an essay of at least 250 words on the topic. Give reasons for your answer and include any relevant examples from your knowledge or experience.

VOCABULARY FOR WRITING: TASK 2 — Describing problems and solutions

No magic bullet

1 Work in groups. Take turns to describe the photos below.
- What problem could the photo illustrate?
- Suggest at least one possible solution.

2a Match the problems, 1-4, to the possible solutions, a-d.

1 One dilemma for many parents is whether to allow their children to access the internet via their smartphones, because they are concerned about the unsuitable content they might be exposed to when using their phones unsupervised.

2 Levels of air pollution in some cities have reached crisis point and pose a serious health risk to people living and working in the worst-affected areas.

3 The link between poverty and poor academic achievement is well known, but it is a complex issue and not one which has a straightforward solution.

4 Local farmers who are struggling to support their families often come into conflict with conservationists as animals stray onto their land and eat their crops or prey on livestock.

a) As well as providing extra support in school for children from disadvantaged backgrounds, it is also important to address the underlying causes of academic underachievement, such as poor housing, poor diet and other broader social problems.

b) One potential means of resolving such disputes is to encourage the local people to become more involved in conservation projects and to help them share in the benefits that wildlife can bring such as through eco-tourism.

c) Government needs to impose stricter regulations and severe financial penalties for companies which continue to pollute in order to force businesses to take their environmental responsibilities more seriously.

d) The problem could, to some extent, be tackled by installing parental control software which blocks access to certain types of sites.

2b Find verbs in the descriptions in exercise 2a which collocate with these nouns.

a) <u>reach</u> crisis point
b) .... a risk
c) .... support
d) .... the causes of (something)
e) .... regulations/penalties
f) .... something seriously
g) .... a problem
h) .... conflict with someone
i) .... a dispute

Vocabulary tip

Using noun phrases is an efficient way to add detail to your writing. When a noun phrase is the subject of a verb, the form of the verb agrees with the 'head noun': Serious air **pollution** in some cities **is** causing an increase in health problems.

2c Find these noun phrases in the descriptions in exercise 2a. In each case, underline the head noun and find the verb it agrees with.

a) One <u>dilemma</u> for many parents *is*
b) Levels of pollution in some cities ....
c) The link between poverty and poor academic achievement ....
d) Local farmers who are struggling to support their families ....
e) One potential means of resolving such disputes ....

VOCABULARY FOR WRITING: TASK 2 — Describing problems and solutions

3a Work in groups. Discuss possible alternative solutions to the problems in 2.

Example: *'Conservationists could work with farmers to build barriers to keep wild animals off their land.'*

3b Present your solutions to the class.

4a Complete the sentences which describe problems. Use one word in each gap.

1. a) Modern consumer culture creates huge amounts of waste which can .... a risk to the environment.

   b) Too much focus on consumer goods can .... social inequality between the haves and have nots.

2. a) It is very difficult for national governments to .... regulations on online advertising, because the content is often hosted abroad.

   b) The amount of online advertising that young people are .... to means that they are sometimes unable to distinguish what is factual content and what is advertising.

3. a) As sea level rises threaten coastal communities in some parts of the world, international governments will be forced to .... climate change seriously.

   b) With the volume of sea ice in the Arctic shrinking every year, some species, such as polar bears, have almost .... crisis point.

4. a) In many parts of the world, teachers are forced to download illegal copies of books because they do not have the resources to .... students with legal copies.

   b) Unless steps are taken to .... the problem of online piracy, smaller publishers may go out of business.

4b Each pair of sentences in exercise 4a looks at a problem from two different perspectives. Identify the perspective in each sentence.

> economic   educational   environmental   legal   political   social

5a Work in groups. Discuss the essay topic below. Make notes on:

- ways to describe/summarize the problem
- possible causes
- possible solutions.

> More than half of the world's population now lives in urban areas. The rapid growth of cities in some parts of the world is bringing all kinds of social, economic and environmental problems.
>
> Describe some of these problems and suggest possible solutions.
>
> Give reasons for your answer and include any relevant examples from your knowledge or experience.

Exam tip

Remember when you are writing about possible solutions, you are not an expert on the subject! The language you use should be tentative.
- Modal verbs:
this approach **could** *help ...,*
better regulation **might** *stop ...*
- Other hedging language:
one **potential** *means of ...,*
to some extent *this would ...*

5b Formulate some of your ideas into full sentences. Remember to use tentative language where relevant.

Example: *Better urban planning might help to create the necessary infrastructure and, in some cases, to anticipate potential problems.*

✎ EXAM TASK: Writing (Task 2)

6 Use some of the ideas from your groupwork in 4 to write an essay of at least 250 words in response to the essay question in 5.

VOCABULARY FOR WRITING: TASK 2 — Expressing opinions

A matter of opinion

1 **Work in groups. Discuss the questions.**

- Do you always carry a mobile phone with you?
- Do you think it's okay to check your phone …
  - when someone is talking to you?
  - when you're being served in a shop?
  - when you're having a meal in a restaurant?
- How would your life be different if you didn't have a mobile phone?

2a **Read the extracts from four student essays in reply to an exam question. What is the opinion of each student?**

> Some people say that we have become too dependent on our mobile phones and that this dependency is having a negative effect on people's ability to communicate face to face. Others, however, say that mobile phones just provide another means of communication that enables us to keep in touch more effectively.
>
> Discuss both these views and give your opinion.

A I don't accept that increased mobile phone usage is having an adverse impact on people's communication skills. Human beings are incredibly versatile and we have the capacity to adapt to new skills without necessarily losing existing abilities.

B It is very apparent in many social situations that people's focus on their mobile devices is incompatible with social relations. Whether they are sitting with friends or at home with their family, all too often people are looking down at their phones rather than talking with the people around them.

C I would argue that whilst people are sometimes distracted by their mobile phones, most people know when it's appropriate to use them and when it isn't. For example, most of us realize that it's impolite to keep checking our phone in the middle of a conversation.

D Personally, I regard mobile phones as just one of the features of modern life that pose a threat to young people's communication skills. As children grow up using instant messaging services, they become incapable of writing in full sentences. Teenagers waste time searching through pages of irrelevant and sometimes misleading content online, but are unable to concentrate on reading a book.

2b **In each extract, underline the word or phrase that introduces the writer's opinion.**

2c **Work in pairs. What is your opinion? Do you agree with any of the views expressed in the extracts?**

3a **Complete the table with the correct noun and adjective forms of the words.**

Noun	Adjective	Noun	Adjective
a)	dependent	compatibility	e) ....
versatility	b)	relevance	f) ....
capacity	c)	appropriateness	g) ....
d)	able	politeness	h) ....

Vocabulary tip

If you are struggling to express an idea in your writing, consider changing the form of a key word, e.g. changing an adjective to a noun.

VOCABULARY FOR WRITING: TASK 2 — Expressing opinions

3b Rewrite the sentences using a different form (noun or adjective) of the word in bold.

a) Plastic is a popular material used in packaging because it is so **versatile**.

Plastic is a popular material used in packaging because of its versatility.

b) Employers are looking for candidates who are **able** to communicate effectively.

c) It is unclear why some people have a particular **capacity** for learning languages.

d) New apps are rigorously tested to ensure **compatibility** with all devices.

4a There are six adjectives used in the essay extracts which have negative prefixes. Underline them.

4b Match the adjectives to the negative prefixes they can be used with.

> appropriate   consistent   ethical   honest   necessary
> probable   reasonable   similar   sufficient

- dis-   • im-   • in-   • un-

4c Choose the best adjective from exercise 4b – with or without its negative prefix – to complete the sentences. More than one answer may be possible.

a) Currently, there is .... evidence to show that mobile phones are harmful to human health.

b) The styles of painting are clearly too .... to be by the same artist.

c) The use of confidential medical data by advertising companies is not only illegal, but ....

d) It is .... to ban advertising of products containing sugar altogether.

e) The risk of exactly the same set of circumstances occurring again seems highly ....

f) Behaviour that is perfectly acceptable amongst friends might be .... in a work context.

5 Work in groups. Take turns to put forward your opinion on the essay topics below.

- Introduce your opinion (*I would argue that …, It seems apparent that …*).
- Explain and give reasons for your point of view (*It's unnecessary/inappropriate …*).
- Give examples from your experience or knowledge where possible.

A

Soft drinks containing high levels of sugar are a major cause of childhood obesity and other health problems. Some people say their sale should be restricted to protect the health of young people. Others argue it is the responsibility of parents to ensure their children eat healthily.

B

Some people argue that popularity of films, TV programmes and other media in English across the world is damaging to local languages and cultures. Others say that a 'global' language enables different cultures to better understand one another.

✎ EXAM TASK: Writing (Task 2)

6 Choose one of the essay topics A or B in exercise 5. Write a paragraph of 3–4 sentences expressing your opinion and giving reasons.

Exam tip

When you are asked to discuss both views and give your opinion, remember that you must make your own opinion clear. Don't just list arguments on both sides.

VOCABULARY FOR WRITING: TASK 2 — Talking about cause and effect

Who's to blame?

1a Work in groups. What are the main causes of arguments within families?

1b Read the sentences below. Did you come up with some of the same issues?

<u>Not sharing your feelings with family and friends</u> can **create** <u>more serious long-term problems</u>.
        CAUSE   EFFECT

a) <u>Many relationship problems</u> **originate from** <u>a lack of communication</u>.

b) <u>Financial issues</u> **are a source of** <u>tension in many families</u>.

c) When underlying tensions already exist, <u>a fairly trivial matter</u> can easily **trigger** <u>a major argument</u>.

d) A <u>change in circumstances</u>, such as a child leaving home, can **prompt** someone to <u>re-evaluate their life</u>.

e) <u>Clothes and appearance</u> **account for** <u>a large proportion of disagreements between teenagers and their parents</u>.

f) <u>Bad behaviour at home</u> can sometimes **stem from** <u>stress at school</u>.

1c Which of the underlined phrases in the sentences in exercise 1b describe a *cause* and which an *effect*?

1d Create paraphrases of some of the ideas in 1a using the sentence halves and linkers below. More than one combination may be possible.

1 Some people keep their feelings hidden from family and friends and …
2 Many problems within relationships are …
3 Tensions within many families are …
4 Lots of arguments between teenagers and their parents are ….
5 Some children can become very stressed at school and …

as a result of
as a consequence
down to
due to
hence

a) problems with money.
b) start to behave badly at home.
c) disagreements about clothing and appearance.
d) they experience more serious long-term problems.
e) poor communication.

2a Work in pairs. Match the possible causes and effects below.

CAUSES	EFFECTS
sedentary lifestyles	air pollution
mass food production	declining wildlife populations
traffic congestion	health problems
healthcare improvements	habitat loss
habitat loss	longer life expectancies

48   TIMESAVER FOR EXAMS: IELTS Vocabulary (5.5–7.5) © Scholastic Ltd.   PHOTOCOPIABLE

VOCABULARY FOR WRITING: TASK 2 — Talking about cause and effect

2b Complete the sentences.

a) One of the consequences of modern sedentary lifestyles
....

b) Mass food production has a major impact on
....

c) The repercussions of habitat loss include
....

d) One result of traffic congestion
....

e) Improvements in healthcare have had positive outcomes
....

> **Vocabulary tip**
>
> When you are describing cause and effect relationships, be careful how you use active and passive verb forms. Using a passive verb form switches the order of the cause and the effect in the sentence.
> *A fairly trivial matter can **trigger** a major argument.* (cause + triggers + effect)
> *Major arguments can **be triggered by** fairly trivial matters.* (effect + is triggered by + cause)

2c Work in pairs. Write five more sentences expressing these cause and effect relationships in different ways. Use a range of different words and structures. Be careful to make the relationships clear.

3 Complete the sentences using a preposition in each gap.

a) There have been severe water shortages in the region as a result .... rapid population growth.

b) A lot of anti-social behaviour stems .... boredom and social exclusion.

c) Three key factors account .... most instances of identity theft.

d) Access to education is one of the primary sources .... social and economic inequality worldwide.

e) The article describes the potential impacts .... climate change .... some of the poorest people in the world.

f) The change to the regulations was prompted .... a number of recent incidents.

> **Vocabulary tip**
>
> Be careful to use these phrases correctly:
> *There have been water shortages **as a result of** rapid population growth.*
> *The population has grown rapidly and **as a result** there have been water shortages.*

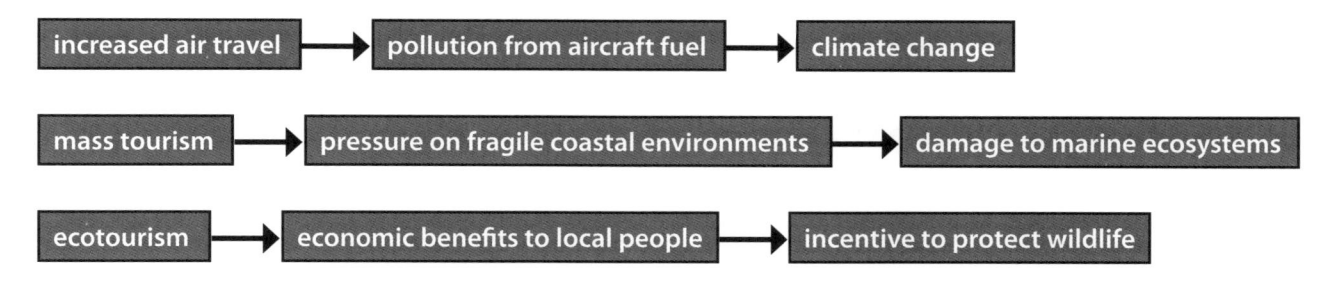

4 Work in groups. Look at the flow diagrams and discuss the cause and effect relationships.

increased air travel → pollution from aircraft fuel → climate change

mass tourism → pressure on fragile coastal environments → damage to marine ecosystems

ecotourism → economic benefits to local people → incentive to protect wildlife

✏ EXAM TASK: Writing (Task 2)

5 Write an essay of at least 250 words in answer to the question below.

> Mass tourism, especially in popular tourist destinations, comes with huge environmental impact. What do you think are the causes and what, if anything, can be done to reduce this impact?

VOCABULARY FOR WRITING: TASK 2 — Giving examples

A case in point

1a Work in groups. Discuss whether you agree with the statements. How significant are these issues in your own country, city or social group?

1 Individuals can do a lot to improve their own health.

2 The 'always-on' culture, where people are constantly connected via smartphones and other devices, can be a significant cause of stress.

3 An important issue for urban planners is reducing traffic congestion.

1b Match examples a–f to the three statements in exercise 1a.

a) The London Congestion Charge and similar schemes provide an example of how vehicles can be discouraged from city centre areas.

b) For instance, people feel obliged to regularly check their work email even when they are at home.

c) Activity monitors are one example of how technology can help encourage a more active lifestyle.

d) The growing problem of online bullying illustrates how social media can be a source of stress for young people.

e) City councils can create infrastructure such as cycle lanes and pedestrianised areas which encourage people to walk and cycle instead of driving.

f) In some cases, very small lifestyles changes, like taking the stairs instead of the lift, may be enough to improve someone's overall health.

1c Underline the words and phrases in a–f in exercise 1b that introduce examples.

VOCABULARY FOR WRITING: TASK 2 — Giving examples

2 Complete the sentences using a word or phrase from the box. More than one answer may be possible.

> cases   example of   example   for instance   illustrates   like   provides   shows   such as

a) Car share schemes are a good .... a simple way to reduce traffic congestion.

b) In many .... people are prepared to leave their cars at home if there is an efficient public transport alternative.

c) People are more likely to exercise regularly if they do something they enjoy, ... playing football with friends.

d) The popularity of tai chi in China .... an interesting example of how people can remain active into older age.

e) Apparently, on average people check social media sites 14 times a day, which .... just how dependent we have become on our online relationships.

f) With so many different ways to keep in touch, ... text messaging, email and social media, people can find it difficult to relax and take time for themselves.

3 Work in pairs. Choose one of the issues in exercise 1a to discuss.

- Which of the examples in exercises 1 and 2 do you think are most interesting and most relevant?
- Which examples can you relate to from your own experience?
- Add more examples from your own experience to support the point.

Exam tip

Task 2 writing questions often ask you to 'include any relevant examples from your knowledge or experience'. Try to include one or two examples to support your main points if possible. Make sure your examples are relevant and clearly linked to the point they support.

4 Work in groups. Take turns to choose one of the topics below. Describe an example from your own knowledge or experience that supports the point.

Communication: What is considered polite in terms of communication differs greatly from culture to culture.	**Sport:** Hosting a major sporting event offers economic, social and cultural opportunities to the host city or country.
Media: Young people can be heavily influenced by the kind of images they see in the media.	**Education:** Technology can have enormous benefits in the classroom.

EXAM TASK: Writing (Task 2)

5 Write a paragraph explaining one of the points from exercise 4. Support the point with a relevant example. Write 3–4 sentences.

VOCABULARY FOR WRITING: TASK 2 — Summarising and concluding

To sum up

1 Work in pairs. Discuss the photos below.
- What type of behaviour does each picture illustrate?
- Is this type of behaviour considered to be a criminal offence in your country?
- What type of punishment do you think is appropriate for these sorts of minor crimes?

2a Read the essay question below and the conclusions of three student essays. Ignore the feedback comments at this stage. Does each student agree or disagree with the statement?

> Putting young people in prison for minor crimes does more harm than good, both for the individuals and for society at large.
>
> To what extent do you agree or disagree?

A

Never? Even for really serious crimes?
Always?
Is this true in every case?

In conclusion, I believe that while it is important to punish young people for their crimes, putting them in prison is not the right answer. Young people who go to prison are easily influenced by more experienced criminals. I would argue that alternative punishments are much better both for the individual and for society.

B

Is this true for even very minor crimes?
What kind of help?

Finding the right balance between punishment and rehabilitation is very difficult. Overall though, I think that it is important to send a strong message to people who break the law. If someone commits a crime, then it is appropriate that they lose their freedom. However, the government should provide help for young people when they come out of prison.

TIMESAVER FOR EXAMS: IELTS Vocabulary (5.5–7.5) © Scholastic Ltd.

VOCABULARY FOR WRITING: TASK 2 — Summarising and concluding

C

Always? In what way?

To sum up, there are clearly strong arguments on both sides of this question. Sending young people to prison is expensive and individuals come out as less useful members of society. Yet, if people believe that their crimes will go unpunished, they will continue to break the law again and again.

2b Underline the words and phrases in the conclusions that introduce a summary.

3 Work in groups. Read the teacher's feedback comments on the conclusions in exercise 2a. Discuss ways you could improve the paragraphs using some of the words and expressions in the box.

> by and large   can be   frequently   in general   in many/most cases
> in many/most contexts   in terms of   may be   often   on the whole

Example: 'In Paragraph A, we could say " … in most cases, putting them in prison is not the right answer".'

Vocabulary tip

Remember:
may be = modal + verb: *Alternative punishments may be better.*
maybe = adverb: *Maybe alternative punishments are better.*

4 In groups, discuss the essay question, using the questions to guide your discussion. Make notes under the headings 'agree' and 'disagree'.

> As we put more and more information about ourselves online, identity theft is becoming a serious global issue. As individuals, it is our responsibility to be careful about what information we share and to protect our personal data.
>
> To what extent do you agree or disagree?

1 What do you know about identity theft?
2 How can individuals protect their personal data?
3 Who else should be responsible for data security and preventing identity theft?

✏ EXAM TASK: Writing (Task 2)

5a Decide your own stance on the topic in exercise 4. Write an outline for an essay, in note form, showing which points from your discussion you would include.

5b Write the concluding paragraph of your essay in full. Summarize your arguments and make your own stance clear. Avoid overgeneralizations. Write around 50 words.

VOCABULARY FOR SPEAKING: PART 1 — Talking about family, friends and home — Collocations

All about me

1a Think of a fact about a friend or relative that you don't think your classmates will know. Write it on a piece of paper.

Example: *My grandfather has an identical twin brother.*
Example: *One of my classmates at primary school lived on a boat.*

1b Work in groups. Put all the pieces of paper in a pile. One person in the group should read out the facts and everyone should try to guess who wrote each fact.

2a Read the comments by two students talking about their family, friends and home. Answer the questions.

1 Why did the two speakers move home?
2 How do they keep in touch with family and friends?

> community   settled in   society   strict   strong   supportive   sympathetic   ~~upbringing~~

A

'I had a fairly sheltered **(a)** *upbringing*. I grew up in a small rural **(b)** .... and my parents are quite conservative. As a teenager, they were pretty **(c)** .... – I studied hard and I helped my mother around the house. I had a small group of close friends, but I didn't go out much. So when I moved to the city to study at university, it was a bit of a shock. At first, I didn't think I was going to fit in, but gradually I got to know some of the other people on my course and after the first few months, I **(d)** .... and really started to enjoy university life. My parents have been amazingly **(e)** .... I'm sure my mum worries about me a lot, but she never lets on. We chat on the phone regularly and she's always positive and encouraging.'

> adapt   adopt   extended   face   located   person   relocated   suburban

B

'I spent my early childhood in a small town on the coast. It was a great place to grow up – I remember long, summer days playing with all the other kids on the beach. Then in my early teens, we **(f)** .... to the city because of my father's job. We moved to a quiet **(g)** .... neighbourhood that, to me, just seemed like the most boring place in the world! At first, I really missed all my old friends, but I think kids **(h)** .... really quickly and I'd soon made lots of new friends at school. I still keep up with a handful of my childhood friends on social media. We share lots of photos and stuff. And when I go back to visit my grandparents and other **(i)** .... family, I can catch up with them in **(j)** .... We hang out at the beach, talk about what we've been up to and just generally have a laugh.'

2b Complete the comments using words from the boxes. Not all the words are needed.

VOCABULARY FOR SPEAKING: PART 1 — Talking about family, friends and home — Collocations

2c Find words or phrases in the comments which have a similar meaning.

a) community – *neighbourhood*   c) adapt – ....

b) relocate – ....   d) supportive – ....

3 Choose the best verb to complete the sentences. Justify your choice.

a) I come from a big family and I *brought / grew* up in a busy household with lots of relatives.

b) When I started at college, everyone seemed so fashionable and streetwise, I didn't think I'd ever *fit / get* in.

c) Of course, I was nervous when I first met my husband's family, but I tried not to *catch / let* on – I smiled and chatted politely.

d) Social media is a great way to *keep / meet* up with family and friends who live abroad.

e) Whenever I visit my home town, I take the opportunity to *make / catch* up with old friends over a coffee.

f) In the summer, I spend most weekends *hanging / staying* out with my friends at the park.

g) I *get / take* on really well with my sister, whenever we get together, we always *have / make* a laugh.

h) When we first moved to New York, I felt pretty lonely and I really *lost / missed* my family and friends back home, but I gradually settled in and *knew / made* new friends.

> **Vocabulary tip**
>
> You say that you *grew up* somewhere to talk about where you spent your childhood. You say that *you were brought up* (often passive) to talk about the way you were taught to behave by your family, your culture, etc. The noun *upbringing* comes from *bring up*.

4a Match the adjectives in the box to the key nouns. Add any other adjectives that fit.

> childhood   good   immediate   large   local   personal   residential   small   social   urban

- COMMUNITY: rural, ...
- LIFE: ...., university
- NEIGHBOURHOOD: suburban, ...
- FRIEND: close, ...
- FAMILY: ...., extended

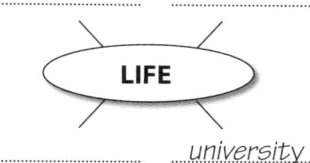

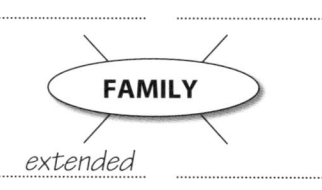

4b Make notes about five things you could say about your own friends, family and home. Use the collocations in exercise 4a.

5 Work in pairs. Note down seven questions that an examiner might ask you about your friends, family and home. Use the prompts to help you.

- Where …? • Do you like/enjoy …? • How often …? • Why …? • How long …? • Who …? • When …?

✎ EXAM TASK: Speaking (Part 1)

6 Work in groups. Take turns to talk for 2 minutes about your family and friends and where you live.

VOCABULARY FOR SPEAKING: PART 1   Talking about work, studies and interests   Phrasal verbs

What are you up to?

1a Rank the interests below from 1 to 6.

1 = an activity you already enjoy or would like to try.   6 = the activity you're least interested in.

walking in the countryside ....   going to the gym ....   online gaming ....

gardening ....   listening to music ....   arts & crafts ....

1b Work in pairs. Compare your lists and explain your choices.

2a Match questions 1–3 to possible responses a–f.

1 What kind of work do you do?   2 Tell me a bit about your studies.   3 What do you do in your free time?

a 'For the past few months, I've been working as a tour guide. I show groups of foreign tourists around the historic sites of Bangkok. I really enjoy meeting so many different people from different countries, but really it's only a temporary job. I'm hoping to go abroad to study Travel and Tourism at university in Australia.'

b 'I'm in the second year of my undergraduate studies at the moment. I'm doing a course in Economics. I'd like to work for an international company one day, so when I graduate, I'm hoping that I'll get the chance to do a Master's in either the UK or the US. I think that studying in an English-speaking country will really improve my career prospects.'

c 'I'm in my final year at university and I'm due to finish my degree, in Food Science, in a couple of months. I've been studying really hard recently. I've been trying to juggle revising for my final university exams and studying for IELTS at the same time. It's all been quite stressful and I'm really looking forward to the summer break now.'

d 'I'm really into running at the moment. I took it up a couple of years ago because I was quite stressed at work and I wanted to do something to help me relax. At first I'd just run a couple of times a week, but then a friend persuaded me to sign up for a 10K race and I started training more seriously. I've taken part in a few 10K events now and I'd like to have a go at running a half-marathon next.'

e 'I work in a primary school, teaching children aged five to seven. It's a fairly small, local school near where I live. The kids are great and it's a really rewarding job.'

f 'I don't have any regular hobbies as such, but recently, I've got involved with a local conservation group. We organize events to help raise awareness about threats to wildlife in our area. We sometimes visit schools to talk to the kids about what we do and we encourage them to join in with activities like collecting litter from local beaches.'

2b Find words or phrases in the students' responses which mean ...

a) only for a short time, not permanent   *temporary*.   e) to try something for the first time ....

b) have the opportunity to do something ....   f) worth doing and giving you satisfaction ....

c) the likelihood of getting a good job ....   g) to educate people about something ....

d) doing two or more things at the same time ....

3 Work in groups. Take turns to describe something in your own life which ...

- you've found rewarding.
- you've had the chance to do.
- is temporary.
- you have to juggle.
- you'd like to have a go at.
- you'd like to raise awareness of.
- might help your career prospects.

VOCABULARY FOR SPEAKING: PART 1 — Talking about work, studies and interests — Phrasal verbs

4a Use the prompts to think of questions about your work or studies. Then use your answers to prepare to talk for one minute.

- Where do you work/study?
- Why …?
- How long …?
- Who …?
- What …?

Exam tip
Try not to give short answers in the first part of the speaking test. Give details and examples. Say what you like or don't like about your job/studies.

4b Work in pairs. Spend one minute telling your partner about your work or studies. Don't interrupt your partner, but listen carefully to what they tell you.

4c Swap partners. Tell your new partner about what your first partner told you.

5 Match the sentence halves. Pay particular attention to the phrases and phrasal verbs in bold.

1 I love surfing, so I always **look**
2 I'm not really into sport, but recently I **took**
3 I really enjoy photography so I've **signed**
4 I'm a member of a tennis club and I **take**
5 If I had the chance, I'd like to **have**
6 For a few years, I've been **involved**
7 The park run events **take**
8 I'm not very good at football, but I **join**

a) **up** for a course to learn a bit more.
b) **part** in quite a few competitions.
c) **with** a local theatre group.
d) **a go** at skiing one day.
e) **place** in a local park every Sunday.
f) **forward to** the summer when I can go to the beach.
g) **in** with my friends when we're at the park.
h) **up** yoga to improve my fitness.

6a Work in groups. Brainstorm things members of the group do in their free time. Use the headings and examples to help you.

Sporting activities
Running

Groups & organized activities
Member of a conversation group

Informal activities with friend
Meeting for coffee

Individual activities
Photography

Vocabulary tip
Remember that when an event *takes place*, it happens. When you *take part* in an activity, you participate. Note that *participate* is a more formal verb used in writing, but not usually in informal speech.

6b In your group, discuss how often you do the activities you noted down. Use some of the words in the box.

> all the time   every so often   from time to time   now and again   occasionally
> once or twice a week   regularly   whenever I can

✎ EXAM TASK: Speaking (Part 1)

7a Prepare answers to the questions below. Don't write a 'script', but you can make notes.

- Tell me a bit about your work/studies.
- What do you like most about your job/studies?
- What do you like to do in your free time?

7b Work in pairs. Take turns to play the role of the examiner and the candidate.

VOCABULARY FOR SPEAKING: PART 1 — Talking about likes and dislikes   Adjectives

Love it or hate it

1 Work in groups. Take turns to share something you like and something you dislike in each category.

- Food
- Films
- Weather
- School subjects
- Sport
- Travel

2a Do the comments below broadly describe likes (L) or dislikes (D)?

a 'At school, I was really fascinated by ancient history, especially the civilizations of Ancient Greece and Egypt. I think it's the idea that people living such a long time ago actually weren't so different from me that appeals to me.'

b 'My brother goes fishing every weekend. I'm afraid I don't see the point of it myself. He just sits by the river in all weathers, getting cold and wet. Then when he does catch something, he throws it back. It just seems like a waste of time to me.'

c 'I'm not a very sporty person, but I'm quite keen on swimming. You don't have to run around getting hot and sweaty, you can just go up and down at your own pace. I find it quite relaxing.'

d 'I'd like to have a career doing something worthwhile, like being a doctor maybe. I think I'd enjoy something working directly with people. I'm slightly put off by how long you have to study for though.'

e 'The thing I really can't bear is going shopping at the weekend. The shops are just packed with people. And it's frustrating when you go from shop to shop and you can't find what you want. I find it really stressful.'

2b Underline the words and phrases which express like or dislike.

3a Match the sentence halves. Think about both form and meaning.

1 From a really young age, I've always been fascinated …

2 I think that things like gardening tend to appeal …

3 To be honest, I don't really see the point …

4 Personally, I've never been very keen …

5 I like to watch films in English, so I find it …

6 I enjoy visiting art galleries, but I can't bear …

a) frustrating that they're often dubbed into German here.

b) to older people more.

c) by animals and by the natural world in general.

d) on fish and other seafood.

e) queuing for hours to get into a really popular exhibition.

f) of travelling abroad just to sit on the beach for a week.

3b Work in pairs. Take turns to make sentences that are true for you.

- I'm fascinated by …
- … seems like a waste of time to me.
- I find … relaxing/stressful, etc
- … appeals to me.
- I'm quite keen on …
- I can't bear …
- I don't see the point of …

TIMESAVER FOR EXAMS: IELTS Vocabulary (5.5–7.5) © Scholastic Ltd.   PHOTOCOPIABLE

VOCABULARY FOR SPEAKING: PART 1 — Talking about likes and dislikes   Adjectives

4 Work in pairs. Do the adjectives express broadly positive or negative opinions? Use a dictionary if necessary. Add one or two more adjectives to each group.

> annoying   dull   exhilarating   fascinating   irritating
> original   pointless   relaxing   stressful   worthwhile

Exam tip
During the speaking test, don't just talk about what you like or don't like, explain why. Use adjectives to describe the positive or negative qualities of something.

POSITIVE

NEGATIVE

5 Complete the sentences using the correct form of the adjective.

a) I read a really *fascinated / fascinating* book about life on an Antarctic research station.

b) We try to create an atmosphere where patients will feel as *relaxed / relaxing* as possible.

c) I find it really *irritated / irritating* when people on the train talk loudly on their mobiles.

d) It's a bit *annoyed / annoying* when you have to queue for ages to get through security.

e) Going up in a hot air balloon is an amazingly *exhilarated / exhilarating* experience.

6 Mark the main stress on the adjectives below.

a) re – **lax** – ing
b) fa – scin – at – ing
c) irr – i – tat – ed
d) ex – hi – lar – at – ing
e) an – noy – ing
f) o – ri – gin – al
g) point – less
h) stress – ful

7a Choose one of the prompts to talk about. Think about how you can describe the experience or activity. Why do you like/dislike it? What positive/negative qualities can you talk about?

- An exhilarating experience
- An activity that you find relaxing
- Something you find irritating
- A stressful situation

7b Work in pairs. Tell your partner about the experience or activity you have chosen. Ask each other questions to find out more.

✎ EXAM TASK: Speaking (Part 1)

8a Work in groups. Choose one of the prompts and brainstorm ideas.

- Fun things to do at the weekend
- Your favourite foods
- The best place to live in your country
- Your favourite type of holiday

Vocabulary tip
If something is *fun*, people enjoy doing it: *We had a fun time at the beach.*
If something is *funny*, it makes you laugh: *He's a really funny guy.*

8b Present your ideas to the class as a group. Talk about what you like and why you like it.

VOCABULARY FOR SPEAKING: PART 2 — Describing anecdotes and past experiences — Colligation

A funny thing happened …

1 Work in groups. Take turns to describe one of the experiences below, but don't say when it happened. Group members should try to guess when.

- Something that happened to you yesterday
- Something you experienced within the last 6 months
- Something you remember from your childhood

2a Match the words in the box to the descriptions. More than one option may be possible.

> a celebration   an event   an experience   a festival   an incident   a memory

a) the Olympic games: ....
b) a party for a 50th wedding anniversary ....
c) a road traffic accident: ....
d) Mardi Gras ....
e) the smell of my grandmother's kitchen ....
f) a year spent living abroad ....

2b Match the student descriptions to the situations in exercise 2a. When did each one happen?

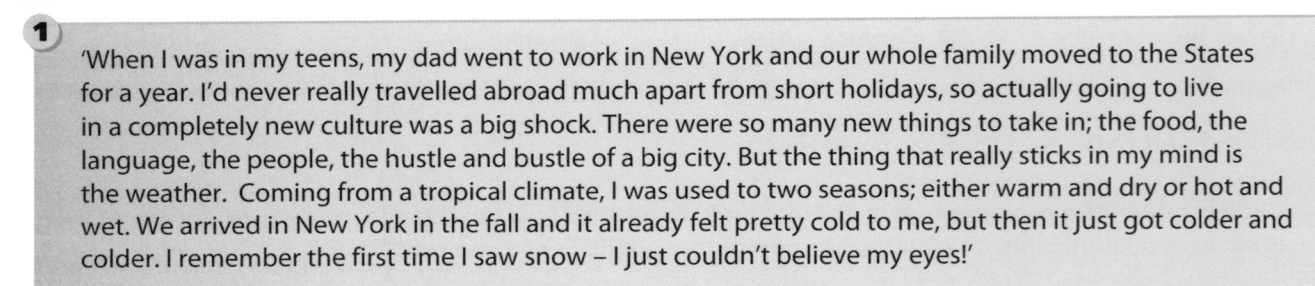

1 'When I was in my teens, my dad went to work in New York and our whole family moved to the States for a year. I'd never really travelled abroad much apart from short holidays, so actually going to live in a completely new culture was a big shock. There were so many new things to take in; the food, the language, the people, the hustle and bustle of a big city. But the thing that really sticks in my mind is the weather. Coming from a tropical climate, I was used to two seasons; either warm and dry or hot and wet. We arrived in New York in the fall and it already felt pretty cold to me, but then it just got colder and colder. I remember the first time I saw snow – I just couldn't believe my eyes!'

2 'I was lucky enough to go to the Olympics when it was in London a few years back. We had tickets for the evening session of the athletics, but we arrived early to soak up the atmosphere in the Olympic Park. I can't tell you how excited I was; milling around through all the crowds of spectators, watching things on the big screens, then making our way into the stadium. The atmosphere was absolutely electric. I took loads of photos of the athletes on the track, but really it's the buzz of the whole thing that I'll never forget.'

3 'Whenever I smell cakes baking, it always takes me back to my childhood and staying with my grandparents. I used to spend the long summer holidays at their place in the countryside. On sunny days, I'd mostly be out in the garden playing with my brothers, but when it rained, I'd go and help my grandmother out in the kitchen. She always seemed to be making cakes and I can vividly remember the wonderful smells and the sweet taste of the cake mixture when she gave me the wooden spoon to lick.'

3 In normal speech, unstressed vowel sounds often become weak /ə/ sounds. Circle any unstressed, weak vowel sounds.

a) incident   b) memory   c) remember   d) summer
e) festival   f) climate   g) atmosphere   h) memorable

TIMESAVER FOR EXAMS: IELTS Vocabulary (5.5–7.5) © Scholastic Ltd.

VOCABULARY FOR SPEAKING: PART 2 — Describing anecdotes and past experiences — Colligation

4 Match the sentence halves. Think about meaning and how the language fits together.

1 I'll never forget …
2 I vividly remember …
3 The one thing that sticks in mind …
4 That theme tune really takes me back …
5 Eating ice cream on the beach always reminds …
6 I think probably my most memorable …

a) all these years later is the nurse who held my hand at the hospital.
b) to my childhood watching TV with my family.
c) me of family holidays when I was young.
d) experience was camping out in the desert under the stars.
e) how I felt the first time I won a race.
f) my first grade teacher calling me up to the front of the class.

5 Choose the best verb.

a) When I opened the box, I couldn't *believe / trust* my eyes!
b) We wandered around just *soaking / taking* up the atmosphere for a while.
c) Everyone was *milling / moving* around in the square waiting for the performance to start.
d) We all *had / spent* an amazing time and came back with loads of great memories.
e) The Glastonbury Music Festival is *held / placed* on a farm in the south of England.
f) I can't *explain / tell* you how upset we all were when the concert was cancelled.
g) The annual parade *holds / takes* place through the streets of the old town.
h) There was so much going on, it was difficult to *soak / take* it all in.

Vocabulary tip

You *remember* something from the past. Something in the present *reminds* you of something from the past.

6a Work in pairs. Tell your partner about a memorable journey. Describe the details of where you went and the transport you used.

6b Swap partners. Retell your story and this time focus on what you saw and heard during your journey.

6c Swap partners again. Retell your story and this time focus on the feelings and emotions you had during the journey.

6d Tell the class what made your journey so memorable.

7 Work in pairs. Read the exam question. Brainstorm ideas for events you could describe. Ask each other extra questions to help generate ideas.

> Describe a large public event you've attended.
>
> You should say:
> - Where and when the event took place
> - What happened
> - Why the event was memorable

Example: 'Who were you with? What was the weather like?'

Exam tip

You will have one minute to prepare for this part of the speaking test. Don't try to write out a 'script'. Instead, write short prompts – key words and phrases.

✎ EXAM TASK: Speaking (Part 2)

8a Work in small groups. Take turns to talk for 2 minutes on the topic in exercise 7.

8b After everyone has spoken, give each other feedback. Say which ideas and images struck you most.

VOCABULARY FOR SPEAKING: PARTS 2 & 3 — Talking about what's typical or general — Exceptions

As a rule

1 Work in groups. Take turns to describe something that's typical in your country for each category.

- Food
- Leisure activities
- Working hours
- Home
- Weather
- School day

2a Read the student comments. Which of the categories in exercise 1 are they talking about?

a 'I'd say that the average family probably lives in an apartment. In the countryside, more people have individual houses, but in urban areas, the vast majority of people live in big apartment blocks.'

b 'Typically, people eat their main meal of the day at lunchtime. Traditionally, people would probably have some kind of noodle dish, but nowadays sandwiches and other more Westernized fast foods are increasingly popular.'

c 'Well, standard office hours are from 8.30 in the morning until 5 in the afternoon. As a rule, though, people work much longer. It's common practice for office workers to stay at their desk until at least 6 or 7 in the evening.'

d 'Because it gets very hot during the middle of the day, schools generally start early in the morning, when it's cooler. Starting school at 7am is pretty much the norm here.'

2b Underline 10 words or phrases in the student comments which describe something that is normal or typical.

3a Do the comments below describe what is typical for ...

- the individual speaker?
- the speaker's city or country?
- another group – who?

> **Vocabulary tip**
>
> If you're asked to talk about what's typical in your country, try to quantify how common it is: *the vast majority of people, increasingly popular*. It will make what you say more interesting and show your range of vocabulary.

a) In Greece, we don't generally have much snow ...

b) On weekdays, I usually get up around 7 o'clock ...

c) In general, older people are less likely to use social media ...

d) As a rule, people here get most of their food from the supermarket ...

e) The normal opening hours for shops where I live are from 9am to 5pm ...

f) On average, I'd say I work about 8 hours a day ...

3b Match the exceptions to comments a–f in exercise 3a.

1 **unless** it's to keep in touch with their grandchildren maybe.

2 **excluding** Sundays.

3 **except** in the far north of the country and in the mountains.

4 **with the exception of** those who live in rural areas and grow their own.

5 **apart from** during the school holidays.

6 that's **not including** my lunch break.

VOCABULARY FOR SPEAKING: PARTS 2 & 3 — Talking about what's typical or general — Exceptions

4a Work in pairs. Take turns to use some of the phrases to talk about things that are true for you or your country. Use topics from exercise 1 or your own ideas.

The average family/student, etc. …	… don't generally …
In China/Spain/Brazil, etc. …	… tend to …
Where I live …	… it's quite common …
As a rule, …	… is increasingly popular …
Traditionally, …	… is the norm …
Typically, …	… is common practice …

4b Can you add any exceptions to your comments in exercise 4a?

Example: *As I said, as a rule, most people eat their main meal at lunchtime, **apart from** during Ramadan when we fast until after sunset.*

5 Read the Exam tip. Work in groups to write four possible follow-up questions for each topic.

1 Describe a TV programme you enjoy watching.
You should say:
- what type of programme it is
- how often it is on
- what happens in the programme

and explain why you enjoy watching this programme.

Example: *What type of TV programmes are most popular in your country?*
How much time do people spend watching TV?

2 Describe a family celebration you enjoyed attending.
You should say:
- what was being celebrated
- how many people were there
- what people did

and explain what you enjoyed about the event.

3 Describe an area of your country you know and like.
You should say:
- where it is
- what its special features are
- what people do in this area

and explain why you like the area.

4 Describe a shopping centre you go to regularly.
You should say:
- where it is
- how often you go
- what kind of shops there are

and explain what kind of shops you like best.

Exam tip

In Part 2 of the speaking test, you are often asked to talk about your own life or experiences. At the end of this section, the examiner will often ask a follow-up question about what's more typical generally. This may help lead into the topic for Part 3.

✎ EXAM TASK: Speaking (Parts 2 & 3)

6a Choose one of the topics in exercise 5. Spend one minute making notes to prepare to talk about it.

6b Work in pairs. Take turns to be the examiner (A) and the exam candidate (B).

A: Introduce the topic: *So can you tell me about …*

B: Talk for at least one minute on the topic using your notes if you want.

A: Ask two of the follow-up questions you prepared in 5.

B: Answer the follow-up questions.

VOCABULARY FOR SPEAKING: PARTS 1, 2 & 3 Talking about what you don't know Adverbials

And then my mind went blank!

1 Which of these topics would you find it easiest to talk about? Rank them from 1 to 10 and explain why.

1 = plenty to say   10 = no ideas!

art ....   business ....   wildlife ....

sport ....   computer gaming ....

music ....   film ....   cooking ....   education ....   science ....

2a Match the questions to the students' responses.

1 Which sportspeople in your country are most popular? ....
2 Do you think downloading music from the internet is becoming more popular? ....
3 What do you think about ecotourism? ....
4 What kind of sporting activities do you enjoy? ....
5 What kind of paintings can you see at the gallery? ....
6 What aspects of air travel do people find stressful? ....

a) 'To be honest, I haven't heard of ecotourism before. I presume it's to do with more environmentally-friendly ways of travelling. Is that right?'

b) 'Personally, I haven't come across this method of accessing music myself. I'm not 100% certain whether people just listen to music online or whether they actually buy songs from the internet.'

c) 'I'm sorry, I can't think of any specific examples off the top of my head. There's a real mix of styles though, from very old masterpieces right through to contemporary works.'

d) 'Actually, I've never flown myself, so I'm not very familiar with the whole process. From what I've seen in films and on TV though, I can imagine there are lots of sources of stress.'

e) 'I'm sorry, my mind's gone completely blank, I can't think of a single name. Football's probably the most popular sport though and lots of footballers have become like celebrities.'

f) 'Well, quite honestly, I'm not particularly keen on sports. I've never really got involved in organized sports activities. I do enjoy yoga though.'

VOCABULARY FOR SPEAKING: PARTS 1, 2 & 3 — Talking about what you don't know — Adverbials

2b Underline the expressions the students use to say they don't know about or aren't interested in the topic.

3 Add the adverbs or adverbial phrases in capitals to the sentences in the most appropriate position.

a) To be honest, I'm not *particularly* interested in art myself. PARTICULARLY

b) I'm not certain how genetically modified foods might affect the environment. ALTOGETHER

c) Actually, I don't know about this area – I've only moved here recently. AN AWFUL LOT

d) I'm not familiar with how online banking works – I haven't used it myself. ESPECIALLY

e) I haven't come across much foreign food – I tend to eat traditional, local dishes. REALLY

f) I have to admit, I've never been to a live sporting event. ACTUALLY

g) I'm afraid I'm not sure what the main ingredients of the dish are. COMPLETELY

h) Personally, I find online computer games boring. A BIT

Exam tip
If a topic comes up that you don't know much about, it's okay to say so, but try to say as much you can about something closely related. Make sure you make the link between the question and your answer clear though. Otherwise the examiner might think you haven't understood the question.

4 Which of these words contain a silent letter at the beginning?

a) knee ✔
b) wrist ....
c) honey ....
d) whole ....
e) where ....
f) honour ....
g) wrap ....
h) knife ....
i) psychology ....
j) khaki ....

Vocabulary tip
Remember, the 'h' in *honest* and *honestly* is not pronounced: /ˈɒnɪst/, /ˈɒnɪs(t)li/

✎ EXAM TASK: Speaking (Parts 1, 2 & 3)

5 Work in pairs. Choose two or three of the topics from exercise 1 which you're <u>least</u> interested in. Write several possible questions on these topics and practise giving answers.

Example:
'What kind of music do you enjoy listening to?'

'To be honest, I don't really listen to an awful lot of music. I do sometimes have music on the radio in the background when I'm studying, but I don't pay much attention to particular bands or singers.'

VOCABULARY FOR SPEAKING: PART 3 — Talking about advantages and disadvantages — Synonyms

The pros and cons

1 Work in groups. Discuss the questions about studying abroad.
- Have you ever studied abroad or would you like to go abroad to study?
- What do you think are the advantages of studying abroad?
- What possible disadvantages are there?

2a Read the comments by four students. Which aspects of studying abroad do they mention?

career   culture   family   language   money

a 'For many people, one of the main motivations for studying abroad is to improve their English. They think they'll benefit from being surrounded by English all the time. From what some of my friends have told me though, in actual fact, many foreign students are so busy trying to keep up with their studies, they spend very little time socialising with English speakers. Instead, they just stick with friends from their own country.'

b 'In theory, I know there are lots of positives to studying abroad, but in practice, I'm put off by the idea of being away from my family for so long. I think I'd really miss them. So for me, the downsides of studying abroad would probably outweigh whatever I might gain from the experience.'

c 'The incentive for many young people to study abroad is to improve their career prospects. A degree from a university in the UK or the US will look great on your CV. Of course, the drawback is that it comes at a cost – studying abroad can be very expensive. So it's down to individuals and their families to weigh up those costs against the potential advantage it will give them in the jobs market.'

d 'Of course, it's a bit of a risk – heading off half way round the world to a place you've never been before. But for me, that's part of the attraction. It's about the adventure and about discovering a new place and a new culture. I think you have to go with an open mind and be prepared to make the most of whatever you come across.'

2b In your groups, note down the advantages and disadvantages of studying abroad that the students mention. Are any the same as the ideas you discussed in exercise 1?

3 Find words or phrases in the comments in exercise 2a with a similar meaning.

a) motivation – *incentive* – ....

b) benefit from – ....

c) in practice – ....

d) advantage – ....

e) downside – ....

Exam tip

Sometimes, paraphrasing the question the examiner asks can give you time to think and help you to concentrate on answering the question. To do this, you need to use synonyms for the words in the question.

VOCABULARY FOR SPEAKING: PART 3 — Talking about advantages and disadvantages — Synonyms

4a Match the sentence halves about the pros and cons of living in a big city.

1 For lots of people, the attraction …
2 People who live in the city benefit …
3 For me, I think the positives of city life definitely …
4 One of the downsides of being in a big city is …
5 City centre apartments are very small, so you have to make …
6 People believe they'll make lots of money, but in actual fact, …

a) the pollution caused by traffic.
b) of living in a big city is the availability of jobs.
c) outweigh the drawbacks.
d) many of the jobs are very poorly paid.
e) from having lots of facilities for sport, education, healthcare.
f) the most of the space you have.

4b Work in pairs. Answer the questions.

1 Which of the statements in exercise 4a describe advantages and which describe disadvantages?
2 To what extent do you agree with the statements?
3 Add two more advantages and two more disadvantages of city life.
4 Do you or have you ever lived in a big city? What is/was your experience like?

Exam tip

Even if you are responding to a very general question, including a personal example in your answer will give you more to say and help to make your answer more memorable.

✎ EXAM TASK: Speaking (Part 3)

5 Prepare a mini-presentation (1–2 minutes), setting out the pros and cons of living in a big city from your own perspective. Include examples from your own knowledge or experience where possible.

VOCABULARY FOR SPEAKING: PART 3 — Expressing opinions — Acknowledging viewpoints

This is what I think ...

1a How strongly held are the opinions expressed below?

a) The speaker feels quite strongly about the topic.

b) The speaker is fairly neutral or doesn't have a strong opinion.

1 'Well, I suppose it's not ideal to fly food halfway around the world, but I guess we're all guilty of buying stuff out of season sometimes.' ....

2 'I firmly believe that sugary drinks should be banned because they're causing incredible damage to young people's health.' ....

3 'Of course, as a pacifist, I'm totally against any kind of violence, no matter how worthy the cause.' ....

4 'I think that boys and girls should be given equal chances in life.' ....

5 'I'm inclined to agree with those people who say that traditional, printed books are better than e-books.' ....

6 'Personally, I don't really approve of people downloading music without paying for it – it's not fair to the musicians.' ....

7 'For my part, I'm a bit sceptical about the idea of banning cars from the city centre – I just don't think it will work.' ....

8 'I know it's an emotive subject, but I'm utterly opposed to keeping animals in zoos – it's cruel and totally unnecessary.' ....

1b Underline the words and phrases which show the speaker's strength of opinion.

1c Do you agree or disagree with the views expressed in 1–8? Rewrite any you disagree with so that they're true for you.

2 In which words is the letter 'o' pronounced /əʊ/ as in go?

approve   choose   chose   emotive   ~~know~~   ~~opinion~~
oppose   propose   purpose   strong   suppose   totally

A /əʊ/ as in go	B a different sound
know	opinion

Exam tip

It's okay to express personal opinions in the speaking test, but try not to become overemotional. Try to express your ideas calmly and give reasons to support your point of view.

3 Work in groups. Take turns to give an opinion in response to the questions. Answer quickly – don't spend too long thinking about your response.

1 Do you think that all young people should go to university?

2 Should smoking in all public spaces be banned?

3 Do you think that a vegetarian diet is healthier than eating meat?

4 Is it realistic for individuals to make changes to their lifestyle in order to protect the environment?

5 Are people really heavily influenced by advertising?

6 Do you think that online shopping is damaging for small local shops and businesses?

VOCABULARY FOR SPEAKING: PART 3 — Expressing opinions · Acknowledging viewpoints

4a Look at the responses to the question and match them to one of the two possible endings, a or b. Think carefully about the position of each speaker.

Do you think children should wear a uniform to school?

1 I **appreciate** that parents get put under pressure to buy kids the latest clothes, so it's probably easier and cheaper for them if they just have to buy one uniform, but …

2 I **recognise** that children, especially teenagers want to express their individual identities, but …

3 To be honest, I can see both sides of the argument, but personally, …

4 I **have to admit** that seeing a whole school of children dressed in the same way does give a good impression, but …

5 I do **sympathise with** kids who don't like wearing a stiff white shirt and a tie every day, but …

a) … I don't think school uniforms are a good idea.

b) … I think school uniforms are a good idea.

4b What is the function of the words and phrases in bold in the comments above?

> **Exam tip**
>
> Sometimes acknowledging the opposite viewpoint before you express your own point of view can make your argument stronger. It will also give you more to say.

4c Think back to your responses in 3. How could you acknowledge the opposite point of view before putting forward your own opinion?

5 Work in groups. Note down possible opinions on both sides of the questions below.

1 Celebrities are often recognized more for their looks than for their actions or opinions. Do you think that's true?

Example:

AGREE	DISAGREE
Lots of 'beautiful' images in magazines	Sports stars celebrated for skills not looks

2 Do you think that the images young people see in the media of perfect-looking celebrities negatively influence the way they feel about themselves?

3 What type of people do you think make the most positive role models for young people?

✎ EXAM TASK: Speaking (Part 3)

6 Work in pairs. Take turns to play the role of examiner (A) and candidate (B).

A: Ask each of the questions in exercise 5 and wait for your partner to answer.

B: Answer the questions giving your own opinion. Try to acknowledge other points of view where necessary and give reasons and examples to support your answers.

VOCABULARY FOR SPEAKING: PART 3 — Talking about what is important — Emphatic adverbs

The important thing is …

1 Work in groups. Read the exam tips and rank them in order of how important you think they are.

1 = the most important
8 = the least important

1 Listen carefully to the examiner's questions. ....
2 Keep calm and don't speak too quickly. ....
3 Say as much as you can in answer to each question. ....
4 Don't worry about your accent, but speak as clearly as possible. ....
5 Express your opinions but don't get overemotional. ....
6 Pay attention to grammatical accuracy. ....
7 Give examples to support your ideas. ....
8 Smile and make eye contact with the examiner. ....

2a Read the comments. Do you agree or disagree with the speakers?

A 'I think it's absolutely vital to listen carefully to the examiner's questions. If you don't catch the question, you might go off on completely the wrong track and it'll be quite obvious to the examiner that you've misunderstood.'

B 'I don't think that accurate grammar is a top priority in the speaking test. So long as any grammatical mistakes don't cause confusion or make you difficult to understand, I think fluency is way more important. It's inevitable that you'll make a few errors here and there – I wouldn't worry about it.'

C 'One of the key things is to keep talking. I don't mean that you should just ramble on about anything, but there's nothing worse than a one-word answer followed by an awkward silence.'

D 'Some people seem to think it's essential to have a perfect British accent. Nothing could be further from the truth! It honestly doesn't matter what kind of accent you have, the crucial thing is that you speak clearly and that the examiner can understand what you're saying.'

2b Underline the words and phrases the speakers in exercise 2a use to stress what is important.

Vocabulary tip

Notice that the word *quite* has different meanings in different contexts:
1 a bit, slightly: *it's quite small, it was quite cold, I'm quite tired.*
2 completely: *it's quite obvious, they're quite different, you're quite right.*

VOCABULARY FOR SPEAKING: PART 3 Talking about what is important   Emphatic adverbs

3 Choose the most appropriate adverb to complete the sentences.

a) In any exam, it's *absolutely / especially* essential that you read the questions thoroughly.

b) For writing tasks, it's *completely / extremely* important to check the word limit.

c) It will be *pretty / totally* clear to the examiner if you've misunderstood the question.

d) Examiners will tell you that it's *completely / quite* evident when an answer is pre-prepared.

e) Most people agree that showing a good range of vocabulary is *absolutely / very* key to getting a high score.

f) There's often *absolutely / very* great pressure on students to do well in exams.

> **Vocabulary tip**
>
> We use adverbs such as *completely* and *absolutely* with limit or extreme adjectives: *completely wrong, absolutely vital.*
>
> We use adverbs like *very, really* and *quite* with gradable adjectives: *really important, quite significant.*

4a Work in groups. Brainstorm tips for someone learning a new language.

Example: *Make sure you note down new vocabulary accurately.*

4b Rephrase your tips to stress what is most important. Use some of the language from exercises 2 and 3.

Example: *'It's absolutely vital that you note down new vocabulary accurately.'*

4c Present your top tips to the class.

✎ EXAM TASK: Speaking (Part 3)

5a Work in pairs, A and B. Read one of the questions below. Spend 1 minute noting down 3 or 4 ideas.

Student A: What do you think young people need to consider when choosing a subject to study at university?

Student B: What do you think are the most important factors when choosing a career?

5b Take turns to explain your ideas from exercise 5a to your partner. Follow the steps.

1 Introduce your topic.

2 Present the ideas you noted down.
- Emphasize the most important points.
- Give reasons and examples where relevant.

VOCABULARY FOR SPEAKING: PART 3 — Expressing uncertainty   Hedging language

The odds are ...

1a Work in groups. How certain do you feel that these things will happen?

10 = 100% certain

5 = maybe, maybe not

1 = highly unlikely

1 People will land on Mars within your lifetime. ....
2 Everyone will be driving electric cars in 10 years' time. ....
3 Print books will be completely replaced by e-books. ....
4 Climate change will significantly affect our way of life. ....
5 People will predominantly study online instead of going to university. ....
6 Water resources will become the main source of conflict around the world. ....

1b Read some responses to the statements in exercise 1a. Underline the words or phrases which show their degree of certainty. How certain do you think each speaker is?

1 'I think there's bound to be a manned mission to Mars sooner or later. Maybe not in the next few years, but probably within, say, the next 20 years.'

2 'It seems unlikely to me that everyone will be driving electric cars in 10 years because the technology's just not cheap enough yet. I would imagine it'll become increasingly common though, at least in more developed countries.'

3 'I think the odds are that certain types of book will be completely digital in the future.'

4 'Apparently, some of the extreme weather we've already been experiencing is due to climate change. So it seems highly likely that's only going to get worse.'

5 'I think it depends what type of subject you're studying. Potentially some subjects could be studied largely online, but I think others, such as languages, will continue to be more popular face-to-face.'

6 'Well, what with climate change and a growing population, presumably water resources will come under more pressure in the future. So, I guess access to water is liable to become a source of conflict.'

VOCABULARY FOR SPEAKING: PART 3 — Expressing uncertainity — Hedging language

Exam tip

When you are expressing ideas that you can't be certain about, remember to use hedging (tentative) language:
- modal verbs: *may, could, might*
- tentative verbs: *seem to, appear to, tend to*
- adjectives and adverbs: *probable/probably, potential/potentially*
- other expressions: *I guess, I imagine, the odds are …*

2 Rewrite the sentences below to make them more tentative by adding the word or phrase in capitals. Make any other changes necessary.

a) It is clear that e-cigarettes could help reduce the harm caused by conventional cigarettes. SEEM

   It seems clear that e-cigarettes could help reduce the harm caused by conventional cigarettes.

b) In the future, more and more everyday tasks will be carried out online. LIABLE

c) Most people would prefer to see a doctor face-to-face rather than filling in an online questionnaire. IMAGINE

d) I believe fossil fuels will eventually run out, but it won't be in my lifetime. ODDS

e) I think that the increase in land needed to farm animals for the growing demand for meat is damaging to the environment. POTENTIALLY

f) Many people already read the news online, but people won't stop reading printed newspapers altogether. LARGELY, UNLIKELY

3 Mark the main stress on these words.

a) pre –(sum)– ably

b) a – ppar – ent – ly

c) po – ten – tia – lly

d) pro – bab – ly

e) seem – ing – ly

f) po – ssib – ly

g) un – like – ly

✎ EXAM TASK: Speaking (Part 3)

4 Work in pairs. Take turns to ask and answer the questions. Give reasons for your answers and give examples where relevant.

1 What changes do you think we will see in school classrooms in the future?

2 How do you think people can be encouraged to change unhealthy lifestyles?

3 Do you think English will continue to be the main global language?

4 How do you think public transport in your area could be improved?

Answers

Reading

All about image (pages 6–7)

2 Rembrandt van Rijn, 1669
   Elisabeth Vigée Le Brun, 1782

3a a) face: facial expression, ageing face
    b) clothes: what you're wearing, clothing, hat, (formal) attire, (fancy) garments
    c) colour: colour scheme, highlights, shadows, rich colours

4   B depict, present
    C original, ingenious
    D particulars, minutiae
    E fragile, flimsy

5   a) scheme b) facial c) realistic d) emotional e) textures f) composition

6   1 a 2 b 3 c

Telling tales (pages 8–9)

2b (suggested answers)
    A a) Parson Weems in the foreground, George Washington in the background (with his father)
    b) The writer of the story (Weems) is opening a curtain to reveal a scene from his own story. The painting illustrates both the story of Weems (who was famous for writing exaggerated stories about Washington) and also the fable about Washington and the cherry tree itself.
    c) Probably not (it was a 'tall tale')
    B a) The handkerchief-tied bundle shows that the boy has run away from home
    b) They are leaning close together talking, the adult characters are smiling
    c) The scene seems to show a time when a young boy away from home would be safe and protected by the adults he meets

3   1 g 2 f 3 h 4 I 5 a 6 c 7 b 8 e 9 d

4   b) narrative c) dialogue d) tall tales e) storybook f) props g) portrayal h) iconic i) nostalgia

5   1 taking place 2 imagery 3 the setting

A matter of perspective (pages 10–11)

2a (suggested answers)
    perspective 2 and dimension 3

2b perspective a 3 b 1
    dimension c 2 d 1

3   (suggested answer)
    They use photographs to help them create paintings with very detailed, complex perspective.

4a a) expectation b) artistic c) composition d) perceive e) symmetrical f) mirror g) geometric h) specificity

4b b) mirrors/mirrored c) geometric d) symmetry e) specify f) expectations g) artists h) composed ('compositions' is also possible)

5   1 T 2 NG 3 F 4 F 5 T

In touch (pages 12–13)

2a (suggested answers)
    Social media (Instagram, Facebook)/online, seeing people in person, telephone, texting

2b (possible answers)
    YES 2 Young people are not forming genuine friendships.
    3 Young people can feel lonely.
    4 When you have problems, you need a real friend, not just friends on social media.
    NO 1 You can keep in touch with friends and family who don't live nearby.
    2 You can stay up-to-date with everyone's news more easily.
    3 Better communication can make friendships stronger.
    4 Young people can share their feelings.

3a a) with b) in c) out d) in e) up f) with g) in h) with

3b 1 a 2 e 3 d 4 b 5 c

4   a) spend b) leave c) keep d) hold e) form/make

5   a) means of communication b) device c) social media platform d) relationship

6   1 A 2 B 3 B 4 D 5 D

Just a game (pages 14–15)

2a How do new sports get added to the Olympic Games?

3a a) fighting b) make c) shine d) make e) has

3b (suggested answers)
    have a fighting chance = have a strong chance of achieving something
    make the leap = to make significant progress
    the chance to shine = an opportunity to show how good you are
    (not) make the cut = not be chosen from among several options
    have a good shot at = have a good chance of succeeding

4a 1 c 2 f 3 g 4 e 5 h 6 a 7 b 8 d

4b (suggested answers)
    below par – golf
    move the goalposts – football
    throw in the towel – boxing
    keep your eye on the ball – any ball game
    a level playing field – usually football
    an own goal – usually football

neck and neck – horse racing
frontrunner – athletics/running or horse-racing

5   1 C 2 E 3 D 4 B 5 B

New to science (pages 16–17)

2b   2 million already identified – another 10 million to 100 million undiscovered

3a   a) Paragraph 3: 'biodiversity – the variety of different species'
      b) Paragraph 4: 'deep sea exploration robots – remotely operated vehicles that would enable us to …'
      c) Paragraph 6: 'deforestation, or clearing away trees'

3b   (suggested answers)
      a) eats rats
      b) is amazingly diverse in terms of biology
      c) biodiversity which have not been explored much
      d) is operated remotely
      e) was not known previously
      f) had not been disturbed before

3c   (suggested answers)
      a striped frog – a frog with stripes
      a rat-eating plant – a plant that can eat rats
      a poisonous, hot pink millipede – a millipede (an insect with a long body and lots of legs) which is bright pink and is poisonous
      a squid worm – a type of worm that lives in the ocean
      a lime-green jumping spider – a spider which is bright green and can jump
      a tiny patch-nosed salamander – a salamander (a type of lizard) which is very small and has a distinctive marking on its nose

4   1 g 2 i 3 f 4 b 5 a 6 e

5   1 15,000 to 20,000 2 2 million 3 10 to 100 million 4 3000 metres 5 poisonous 6 (the) Philippines 7 spider 8 2008 9 Georgia 10 2007

Caffeine kick (pages 18–19)

2a   (suggested answer)
      They present the drinks as being 'healthy' when in fact, they may be harmful to health.

2b   a) ads b) boost, lift c) plunge d) guzzle

3a   (suggested answer)
      The drinks can cause hyperactivity the symptoms of which (lack of concentration, anxiety, lack of sleep) might affect school performance.

3b   a) consume b) anxiety c) disrupted sleep d) kids

3c   a) 'consume' is more formal than 'eat or drink'
      b) 'anxiety' is slightly more formal than 'worry'
      c) 'insomnia' is a more formal, medical term for 'disrupted sleep'
      d) 'children' (which is neutral) is more formal than 'kids' (which is informal)

5   a) recommendation b) side effect
      c) diagnosis d) symptoms

6   1 C 2 F 3 A 4 B 5 H

Out of this world (pages 20–21)

1a   a) biologist b) engineer c) chemist d) physicist
      e) pharmacologist f) astronomer g) geneticist h) geologist

2a   1 D 2 C 3 A 4 B

2b   b) observations c) hypothesis d) exists

3   (suggested answers)
      a) if it exists, it could be a big one; should be around 10 times the mass of Earth; orbit the sun at an average distance of around 25 times as far as Neptune; may be an ice giant; its orbit is very elliptical; hasn't always been exiled to the outer reaches of the solar system; it formed near Jupiter and Saturn; probably got flung out to the solar system's hinterlands
      b) observations of the objects with weird orbits in the Kuiper belt are the only evidence for Planet Nine's existence

4   1 Y 2 NG 3 Y 4 N 5 N 6 NG

Crash test dummies (pages 22–23)

2a   a) Parts of the body: torso, legs, head, neck, ribs, chest
      b) Vehicle safety features: airbags, seat belts

2b   (suggested answer)
      An undistracted driver

2c   a) accelerometers monitor the speed and direction of the head as it slows after impact
      b) torque, or twisting force
      c) compression … These measurements predict the risk of broken ribs

3a   b) batter, pummel c) sensor d) impact e) severity
      f) measure, monitor g) performance h) manufacturer

3b   a) severity b) sensors c) design / performance
      d) manufacturers e) performance / design f) monitor / measure g) impact h) battered / pummelled

4   Paragraph 2

5   1 the severity of 2 experiences 3 of the chest 4 stored in

A way of life (pages 24–25)

2   a) The Sami people
      b) Lapland, Northern Finland
      c) To follow their animals/reindeer as they migrate
      d) human impact on the environment (climate change, mining, logging)

3a   1 c 2 d 3 b 4 a

3b   (suggested answers)
      A custom is something that people in a particular group or culture typically do, such as shaking hands when they meet.

Answers

Tradition is a more general word that includes things which people do, things they believe, etc. and which have been the same for many years.

Someone's livelihood is anything they do to make money to live; including, for example, herding reindeer, farming, fishing, etc. A job is usually when someone works as an employee for a particular company.

We typically use way of life to talk about all the circumstances around how someone lives; where they live, their work, their free time, etc. We more often use lifestyle to talk about the choices individuals make about how they live; what they eat, what they do in their free time, etc.

4   a) threat b) survive c) culprit d) keep
5   1 C 2 D 3 A 4 E 5 B
6   b) wilderness c) pristine d) fragile e) advocate
7   1 (the) Sami 2 60 kilometres per hour 3 the Arctic tundra 4 3,000 years ago 5 20 6 meat / food 7 human intrusion 8 stronger laws

Crime fighters (pages 26–27)

3   b) roadblocks c) patrol d) armed backup e) the presence of f) protect
4a b) stopping – doing c) to stop – to do d) killing – doing e) save – do f) protecting – doing
4b a) to break in b) (to) identify c) leaving d) liaising e) to raise
5   1 F 2 I 3 H 4 D 5 B 6 C

Making music, making money (pages 28–29)

2   (suggested answers)
    a) cassette tapes, CDs, hard-copy recordings, physical formats, records
    b) digital files, downloads, MP3s, platforms, streaming
    c) albums, singles, songs
3a a) skyrocketed, soared b) declined, shrunk
3c a) downward b) downward c) upward d) downward e) upward f) upward
4   a) profit b) salary c) the minimum wage d) revenue e) income f) money
5   B, D, G
6   A, E, F

Writing

Figure it out! (pages 30–31)

1   **Question 1: 1** bar chart **2** graph **3** pie chart **4** table **5** diagram
    Question 2: (suggested answers)
    1 How much land is needed to produce different types of meat
    2 The growth of the world's population between 1800 and today plus the projected growth up to 2100
    3 The distribution of the world's population by continent
    4 The life cycle of a sea turtle
    5 Average life expectancies for men and women in different countries across the world
2   **A** vertical axis **B** horizontal axis **C** solid line **D** dotted line **E** curve **F** segment **G** row **H** column
3   1 b 2 f 3 d 4 a 5 c 6 e

Pick a number (pages 32–33)

1   a) 8,740,000 b) 80 c) 547 d) 1,993 e) 5.2 f) 250,000,000 g) 1630 h) 450 j) 3,600
3   b) (young) people aged 11 to 20 years old c) a two-year study d) a 547-hectare area e) an illness borne by mosquitoes f) a 420-kilogram fungus
4a b) percentage c) range d) amount e) number f) rate g) estimate h) maximum i) minimum j) period
4b b) percentage/number c) majority, number d) amount, period e) range f) rate g) maximum

Trending (pages 34–35)

1a a) Overall upward trend b) No c) 2004-2014 d) Overall downward trend e) Yes, there was an unusual spike from 1988 to 1991 f) Overall downward trend g) No overall trend h) Yes, in 1996 (and possibly 2013) i) Fluctuate. Possible factors: short-term factors such as weather conditions might cause shrimp catches to go up and down each year.
2   a) quantity (not number) b) trend c) upward d) reaching e) peak f) rose g) steadily h) growth
3a Verbs: expand, fall, grow, improve, reduce, rise, shrink
    Adverbs: drastically, fast, gradually, sharply, steadily
3b a movement upwards: expand, grow, improve, rise
    a movement downwards: decline, fall, reduce, shrink
    a slow change: gradually, steadily
    a large change: dramatically, drastically, fast, sharply
3c usually transitive: reduce
    usually intransitive: grow, shrink
    always intransitive: rise, decline, fall
    both: improve, expand

4a (suggested answers)
b) The number of local cinemas has declined gradually.
c) The company has seen/experienced fast growth in Asia.
d) The new design will bring/mean/result in a drastic reduction in energy costs.
e) There is a sharp rise in flu cases in the winter months.
f) Students' average exam grades at the school have improved steadily.

The same but different (pages 36–37)

2a a) Europe and North America; around 46-47% b) Cultural c) About 12-13% d) About 18% e) In the Arab States
2b 1 c 2 a 3 f 4 e 5 b 6 d
3 (suggested answers)
b) Compared with the rest of Spain …
c) … drinks contain an equivalent amount of sugar.
d) … contain only 5 grams of sugar per 100 grams as opposed to 11 grams in the standard drinks. Or … contain only 5 grams of sugar per 100 grams as opposed to the standard drinks which contain …
e) There's still a significant gap between the numbers of boys and girls participating in sport.
f) In urban areas, approximately 95% of homes …
g) In contrast, in rural areas as few as 53% of households have …
h) … scored the highest overall, with/scoring an average of 76% and 81% respectively.
4 (suggested answers)
a) The Chicago coyote
b) Early in the morning and late at night.
c) 3am
d) 7 thousand metres
e) It's less safe to move around in daytime, it's less easy to hunt their prey in daylight.
f) It has to move further to find food.

What comes next? (pages 38–39)

1a C
2a Description A: d, e, b, a, c
Description B: d, b, e, f, a, c
3 Description A
a A **c** A **d** B, B **e** B
Description B
b B **c** B, B **d** both **e** A

In your own words (pages 40–41)

1a a) Fig 2 b) Fig 1 c) Fig 1 d) Fig 2
1b (some possible answers)
a) work/find jobs/are employed/pursue careers
b) study/choose (to study)/graduate in/earn degrees in
c) study/choose (to study)/graduate/get degrees in … choose
d) find work/follow a career/are employed

2a (suggested answers)
a) access, browse, search, use + **the internet**
b) buy, download, listen to, make, purchase, stream + **music**
c) buy, launch, make, market, purchase, sell, use + **a product**
d) earn, make, raise, receive + **money**
2b (suggested answers)
a) launched
b) download (listen to and stream don't work with the preposition 'onto' their mobile phone)
c) listen to/purchase/buy
d) browse/search ('use' is possible but less specific)
e) receive/earn/make ('make' is the least specific verb here)
f) access (browse and search are also possible but describe more specific actions than referred to here)
g) purchase/buy
h) raise

Who's who? (pages 42–43)

2a (suggested answers)
1a) **Work & career**: staff, experts, professional, workers, workforce, employer, employees
b) **Family**: spouse, partner, relatives
c) **Society**: local residents, ethnic groups, migrants, communities, members of the public, neighbours,
2 **No clear group**: consumer, individual, age group
2b (suggested answers)
Individuals: local resident, migrant, expert, member of the public, professional, consumer, neighbour, spouse, partner, individual, relative, worker, employer, employee
Groups: ethnic group, community, age group, staff, workforce
4a b) typical c) stereotypes d) traditionally e) general
f) everyday
5a 1 a, b, c
2 d, e, f
5b (suggested vocabulary from the exercise and questions)
a) sports stars, celebrities, sportspeople, professional, fans, (attract) public attention, the media, (act as positive) role models, stereotypes, teenager, twenty-something, at a young age
b) society, the elderly, older population, the family, immediate family, the general public, retirement age, volunteers, (provide) company, contact with people, caring responsibilities

No magic bullet (pages 44–45)

2a 1 d 2 c 3 a 4 b
2b b) pose c) provide d) address e) impose f) take g) tackle
h) come into i) resolve

Answers

2c **b)** <u>Levels</u> of pollution in some cities + have reached (+ and pose)
c) <u>The link</u> between poverty and poor academic achievement + is
d) <u>Local farmers</u> who are struggling to support their families + come
e) <u>One potential means</u> of resolving such disputes + is

4a **1a)** pose **1b)** create/cause **2a)** impose **2b)** exposed **3a)** take **3b)** reached **4a)** provide **4b)** tackle/address

4b (suggested answers)
1a) environmental **1b)** social **2a)** legal/political **2b)** social/educational **3a)** political **3b)** environmental **4a)** economic/educational/legal **4b)** economic/legal

A matter of opinion (pages 46–47)

2a **A** Mobile phones do not have a negative effect
B Mobiles can have a negative effect
C Mobiles mostly do not have a negative effect
D Mobiles do have a negative effect

2b **A** I don't accept that … **B** None **C** I would argue that …
D Personally, I regard

3a **a)** dependence **b)** versatile **c)** capable (incapable) **d)** ability **e)** compatible (incompatible) **f)** relevant (irrelevant) **g)** appropriate (inappropriate) **h)** polite (impolite)

3b (suggested answers)
b) Employers are looking for candidates with the ability to/who have the ability to communicate effectively.
c) It is unclear why some people are particularly capable of learning languages.
d) New apps are rigorously tested to ensure they are compatible with all devices.

4a incompatible, impolite, incapable, irrelevant, misleading, unable

4b **dis-** dishonest, dissimilar
im- improbable
in- inappropriate, inconsistent, insufficient
un- unethical, unnecessary, unreasonable

4c **a)** insufficient **b)** dissimilar **c)** unethical / inappropriate
d) unreasonable / unnecessary / inappropriate
e) improbable **f)** inappropriate

Who's to blame? (pages 48–49)

1c **a)** effect – originate from – cause
b) cause – be a source of – effect
c) cause – trigger – effect
d) cause – prompt – effect
e) cause – account for – effect
f) effect – stem from – cause

1d **1)** as a consequence / hence + d
2) down to / due to / as a result of + e /a
3) down to / due to / as a result of + a /e
4) down to / due to / as a result of + c
5) as a consequence / hence + b

2a (suggested answers)
sedentary lifestyles – health problems
mass food production – habitat loss
traffic congestion – air pollution
healthcare improvements – longer life expectancies
habitat loss – declining wildlife populations

2b (suggested answers)
a) One of the consequences of modern sedentary lifestyles is health problems.
b) Mass food production has a major impact on habitat loss.
c) The repercussions of habitat loss include declining wildlife populations.
d) One result of traffic congestion is air pollution.
e) Improvements in healthcare have had positive outcomes on life expectancies.

3 **a)** of **b)** from **c)** for **d)** of **e)** of, on **f)** by

A case in point (pages 50–51)

1b **1** c,f **2** b,d **3** a,e

1c **a)** provide an example of **b)** For instance, **c)** are one example of **d)** illustrates how **e)** such as **f)** In some cases, like

2 **a)** example of **b)** cases **c)** for instance / such as / like
d) provides **e)** shows / illustrates **f)** such as / like

To sum up (pages 52–53)

2a **A** agree **B** disagree **C** unclear
2b **A** In conclusion **B** Overall **C** To sum up

3 (suggested answers)
A … Young people who go to prison can be easily influenced by … I would argue that in general alternative punishments …
B If someone commits a crime, then in most cases it is appropriate … the government should provide help in terms of education or training for young people …
C … and individuals frequently come out as less useful members of society because the stigma of a criminal record prevents them from getting work. Yet … On the whole, I believe that in all but the most serious cases, young people should be kept out of the prison system and alternatives such as community service are generally more effective.

Speaking

All about me (pages 54–55)

2a (suggested answers)
1 A to go to university, B because his father relocated for his job
2 A phones her mother regularly, B uses social media to keep in touch with old friends

2b b) community c) strict d) settled in e) supportive f) relocated g) suburban h) adapt i) extended j) person

2c b) move c) fit in d) (positive and) encouraging

3 a) grew b) fit c) let d) keep e) catch f) hanging g) get, have h) missed, made

4a (suggested answers)
rural, local, small, urban COMMUNITY
university, personal, social LIFE
suburban, local, residential, urban NEIGHBOURHOOD
close, childhood, good FRIEND
extended, immediate, large, small FAMILY

What are you up to? (pages 56–57)

2a 1 a, e 2 b, c 3 d, f

2b b) get the chance to do (something) c) career prospects d) juggle e) have a go at (something) f) rewarding g) raise awareness of (something)

5 1 f 2 h 3 a 4 b 5 d 6 c 7 e 8 g

Love it or hate it (pages 58–59)

2a a) L b) D c) L d) both e) D

2b (suggested answers)
a) fascinated by, appeals to
b) don't see the point of, seems like a waste of time
c) quite keen on, find it quite relaxing
d) worthwhile, enjoy, slightly put off by
e) really can't bear, frustrating, find it really stressful

3a 1 c 2 b 3 f 4 d 5 a 6 e

4 **Positive**: exhilarating, fascinating, original, relaxing, worthwhile
Negative: annoying, dull, irritating, pointless, stressful

5 a) fascinating b) relaxed c) irritating d) annoying e) exhilarating

6 b) FAscinating c) IRRitated d) exHIlarating e) anNOYing f) oRIginal g) POINTless h) STRESSful

A funny thing happened (pages 60–61)

2a (suggested answers)
a) an event b) a celebration c) an incident d) a festival e) a memory f) an experience

2b 1) f, in the speaker's teens 2) a, in 2012
3) e, in the speaker's childhood

3 (suggested answers)
b) mem<u>o</u>ry c) remem<u>b</u>er d) summ<u>e</u>r e) festiv<u>a</u>l f) clim<u>a</u>te g) atmosph<u>e</u>re h) mem<u>o</u>rable

4 1 f (e) 2 e (f) 3 a 4 b 5 c 6 d

5 a) believe b) soaking c) milling d) had e) held f) tell g) takes h) take

As a rule (pages 62–63)

2a a) Home b) Food c) Working hours d) School day

2b (suggested answers)
a) average, the vast majority of
b) typically, traditionally, increasingly popular
c) standard, as a rule, common practice
d) generally, the norm

3a a) the speaker's city or country
b) the individual speaker
c) another group – older people
d) the speaker's city or country
e) the speaker's city or country
f) the individual speaker

3b 1 c 2 e 3 a 4 d 5 b 6 f

And then my mind went blank! (pages 64–65)

2a 1 e 2 b 3 a 4 f 5 c 6 d

2b (suggested answers)
a) To be honest, I haven't heard of ecotourism before.
b) Personally, I haven't come across this method of accessing music myself. I'm not 100% certain whether people …
c) I'm sorry, I can't think of any specific examples off the top of my head.
d) Actually, I've never flown myself, so I'm not very familiar with the whole process.
e) I'm sorry, my mind's gone completely blank, I can't think of a single name.
f) Well, quite honestly, I'm not particularly keen on sports. I've never really got involved in organized sports activities.

3 (suggested answers)
b) I'm not altogether certain …
c) Actually, I don't know an awful lot about this area …
d) I'm not especially familiar with …
e) I haven't really come across …
f) Actually, I have to admit … OR … I've never actually been to …
g) … I'm not completely sure …
h) Personally, I find online computer games a bit boring.

4 a, b, d, f, g, h, i
The w is pronounced in where, but the h is silent.
The k is pronounced in khaki, but the h is silent.

Answers

The pros and cons (pages 66–67)

2a (suggested answers)
a) language b) family c) career, money d) culture

2b (suggested answers)
Advantages: improving your English, improving career prospects, discovering a new place and a new culture
Disadvantages: no time to socialise with English speakers, missing family, cost, risk of the unknown

3 a) attraction b) gain from c) in actual fact d) positive (n) e) drawback

4a 1 b 2 e 3 c 4 a 5 f 6 d

4b Question 1:
Advantages: 1, 2, 3
Disadvantages: 4, 5, 6

This is what I think ... (pages 68–69)

1a (suggested answers)
1 b 2 a 3 a 4 b 5 b 6 b 7 b 8 a

1b (suggested answers)
1 I suppose (it's not ideal), I guess **2** I firmly believe **3** I'm totally against, no matter how (worthy) **4** I think that **5** I'm inclined to agree **6** Personally, I don't really approve of **7** For my part, I'm a bit sceptical about, I just don't think **8** I'm utterly opposed to

2 A: know, chose, emotive, oppose, propose, suppose, totally
B: opinion, approve, choose, purpose, strong

4a 1 a 2 b 3 either 4 a 5 b

4b To acknowledge the opposing argument

The important thing is ... (pages 70–71)

2b (suggested answers)
A absolutely vital, completely (the wrong track), quite obvious
B (not) a top priority, way more important, it's inevitable that
C One of the key things is, there's nothing worse than
D it's essential, Nothing could be further from the truth, honestly (doesn't matter), the crucial thing is

3 a) absolutely b) extremely c) pretty d) quite e) absolutely f) very

The odds are ... (pages 72–73)

1b 1 there's bound to be (certain), maybe not ... but probably (slightly less certain)
2 It seems unlikely to me, I would imagine (not very certain)
3 I think the odds are (fairly certain)
4 Apparently (not very certain), it seems highly likely (fairly certain)
5 I think it depends (aware of more than one possibility), potentially ... could (not very certain)
6 presumably (fairly certainly), I guess (not very certain),

2 (suggested answers)
b) In the future, more and more everyday tasks are liable to be carried out online.
c) I'd imagine most people would prefer ...
d) ... but the odds are it won't be in my lifetime.
e) Potentially, I think ... OR I think that potentially the increase ... OR ...for meat is potentially damaging to ...
f) Many people already read the news largely online, but it is unlikely that people will stop reading ...

3 b) aPPARently c) poTENtially d) PRObably e) SEEMingly f) POssibly g) unLIKEly